THE TOMB AND BEYOND

To John, Ivy, Natalie and Jamie with love

Front cover: A scene from the tomb of Saroy at Thebes
Back cover: A scene from the tomb of Sennedjem at Thebes

THE TOMB AND BEYOND
BURIAL CUSTOMS OF EGYPTIAN OFFICIALS

Naguib Kanawati

Aris & Phillips Ltd – Warminster – England

ISBN 0 85668 734 0

British Library Cataloguing-in-Publication Data
A catalogue record of this book is available from the British Library

Printed and published in England by Aris & Phillips Ltd, Warminster, Wiltshire BA12 8PQ

Contents

MAP OF EGYPT

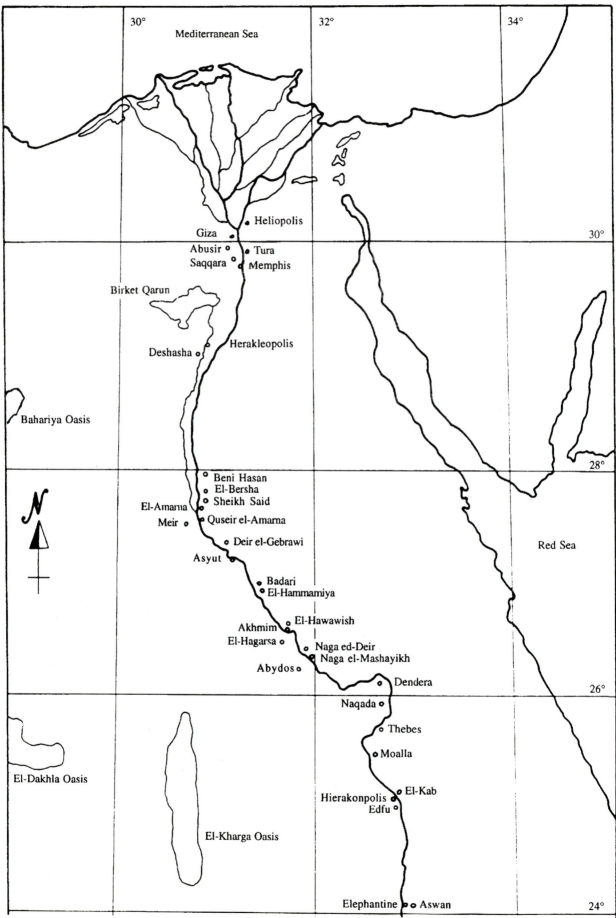

Preface

The tombs, with their scenes, inscriptions, objects and human remains, represent our richest source of information for the understanding of Egyptian funerary beliefs and practices, art and architecture and indeed of various aspects of daily life. While detailed, scholarly reports on individual tombs are abundant, the need existed for a more general work to introduce the lay person and the student to these important and fascinating 'records' of Egyptian civilisation and to render the interpretation of the information found in them more accessible. An abridged form of this work was published in 1987 by the Egyptian Ministry of Culture in its Prism Archaeological Series, under the title *The Tomb and its Significance in Ancient Egypt;* but it soon became apparent that a fuller treatment of the subject was necessary, particularly with regard to the Egyptian concepts of death and the hereafter, hence the present book.

To make the book more useful the reader is presented, whenever possible, with the sources - literary, architectural or artistic - on which the discussions of various ideas are based. While most of the textual quotes have been examined in the original language, it is a pleasure to acknowledge my indebtedness to the excellent translation of these texts by M. Lichtheim (*Ancient Egyptian Literature: A Book of Readings*, 3 vols. [Los Angeles, 1973-80]). Extensive use of illustrations was made, both in line drawings and photographs. Scenes were selected from tombs in different sites as well as from papyri and objects in museums in order to treat all the relevant themes and to cover all periods. Nevertheless, whenever possible a deliberate preference was given to the use of evidence from tombs which I have excavated and/or recorded in various sites in the past twenty years. I hope that my more intimate understanding of these tombs would justify the choice.

It is a particular pleasure to express my deep appreciation to many individuals and institutions for their help and co-operation during the preparation of the book:
Mr. Sameh Shafik (Sohag, Egypt) produced all the intricate and graceful line-drawings published here, from originals acknowledged in the list of figures. **Mr. Naguib Victor** (Sydney, Australia) was responsible for all the detailed architectural drawings, redrawn from acknowledged originals. I would also like to sincerely thank the following for kindly providing me with photographs to complement those from my personal collection: **Mrs. Leonie Donovan** for the cover photographs and for plates 10, 11, 20, 29, 30, 41, 42, 47-52, 55, 61-63, the **British Museum** for plates 23-26, 28, 31, 59, the **Egyptian Museum, Cairo** for plates 5, 12, 14, 21, 22, and the **Museum of Ancient Cultures,** Macquarie University for plate 16.

During the preparation of this book I received assistance from many individuals in the form of reading the manuscript and suggesting improvements. In that respect I would like to express my appreciation to Miss Joan Beck, Mrs. Kim McCorquodale, Dr. Ann McFarlane, Mrs. Joan Pollett and Mrs. Elizabeth Thompson. My special thanks go to Miss Kim Wilson and Mrs. Elizabeth Thompson for their care and patience in the preparation of this book for printing, the former for her work on the text and the latter on the artwork.

Naguib Kanawati
Macquarie University
Sydney, Australia

CHRONOLOGY

The dates listed below are mainly based on the work of J. von Beckerath, *Chronologie des pharonischen Ägypten* (Mainz am Rhein, 1997). All dates before the Late Period are approximate and particularly those before the beginning of the Middle Kingdom, where the figures reached by different scholars vary considerably. In setting the beginning and end of each dynasty before the Middle Kingdom von Beckerath allows for 50 years as a margin of error up or down. His lower limits are adopted here, although our research in the Teti cemetery suggests shorter reigns for kings of the transitional period between Dynasties 5-6 (N. Kanawati - M. Abder-Raziq, *The Teti Cemetery at Saqqara,* vol. 6 [Warminster, 2000]).

The reign of Akhenaten of Dynasty 18 is frequently referred to in the text as the Amarna Period and Dynasties 19 and 20 as the Ramesside Period.

Predynastic Period
Badari, Naqada I-III and Dynasty 0
                                    4500-2982

Early Dynastic Period
Dynasty 1   2982-2803
Dynasty 2   2803-2657

Old Kingdom
Dynasty 3   2657-2589
Dynasty 4   2589-2454
Dynasty 5   2454-2297
Dynasty 6   2297-2166
Dynasties 7-8   2166-2120

First Intermediate Period
Dynasties 9-10 (at Herakleopolis)
                                    2120-2020
Dynasty 11 (at Thebes) 2119-2046

Middle Kingdom
Dynasty 11 (in all Egypt) 2046-1976
Dynasty 12   1976-1793

Second Intermediate Period
Dynasty 13   1793-1645
Dynasty 14 (contemporary with 13)
                                    1645
Dynasty 15 (Hyksos) 1645-1536

Dynasty 16 (Hyksos vassals
      contemporary with 15)
Dynasty 17 (Egyptian rulers at Thebes
      contemporary with 15)

New Kingdom
Dynasty 18   1550-1292
Dynasty 19   1292-1185
Dynasty 20   1185-1069

Third Intermediate Period
Dynasty 21   1069-945
Dynasty 22 (Libyan)   945-730
Dynasty 23 (Libyan)   756-712
Dynasty 24   740-712
Dynasty 25 (Kushite) 746-655

Late Period
Dynasty 26   664-525
Dynasty 27 (Persian) 525-401
Dynasty 28   401-399
Dynasty 29   399-380
Dynasty 30   380-342
Dynasty 31 (Persian) 342-332

Ptolemaic Period
Macedonian Dynasty   332-305
Ptolemaic Dynasty   305-30

Roman Period   30 BC-395 AD

Introduction

To most civilisations a tomb is simply a place to conceal a corpse, but to the ancient Egyptian it was a house for eternity. Such contrasting views are based on completely different concepts of death itself; for while to most cultures this represents an end to a person's earthly association, to the Egyptian the dead enjoyed a kind of continued existence, not only in the Netherworld, but also in the land of the living. According to Egyptian beliefs the individual possessed multiple entities which after death experienced different destinies, in the tomb, in the Netherworld and on earth. Thus despite the presence of the fertile Field of Reeds in the Hereafter, an individual's needs for sustenance from the products of the earth do not end with his death. As a result, the Egyptians, each according to his means, planned for the fulfillment of such future needs by establishing funerary estates and setting up wills to guarantee perpetual supplies. In addition, they supplicated the living to present them with offerings of food and drink, or merely to pronounce 'invocation offerings' for them. The deceased was even able to revisit places he enjoyed during his lifetime, to see the light and even to copulate.

This bond between the dead and the land of the living was fundamental in shaping the principles underlying tomb construction. Since the deceased was believed to have continued some sort of earthly ties, he needed an everlasting earthly dwelling, which was sometimes designed like a contemporary house, only built, whenever possible, of more durable materials. Although we call these buildings 'tombs', there is no indication of their mortuary character in the various Egyptian terms referring to them. A term frequently used for the tomb is *is*, which could equally mean 'council chamber'. Even the burial chamber itself *khenet* is close in its writing to *khenu* which means 'Residence' or 'interior' and *khen* which means 'tent', only the former uses a determinative of a building while the latter, understandably, uses that of a cloth. With regard to decoration, and until well into the New Kingdom, all the scenes depicted in tombs represented the activities of daily life. These scenes were gradually replaced in later tombs by scenes of the Hereafter, which presumably reflects more a change in the Egyptian's view of the tomb than a change in his funerary beliefs.

Tombs consisted of two main sections, a chapel above ground where the deceased's cult was maintained and offerings presented, and a burial chamber where the body was deposited. While the emphasis in size and amount of decoration was on the chapel in the earlier period, this changed to the burial chamber in the later period. Such a change presumably reflects a more practical view of the tomb, after the Egyptian observed the neglect and destruction of chapels through the centuries. However, despite his realisation of the vulnerability of tombs and at times his questioning of their worth, at no time did the Egyptian spare any effort or cost in constructing his own. From the time man settled in the Nile valley to the end of ancient Egyptian history, evidence suggests an unshaken belief in a life after death; both in periods of stability and of relative disorder. Even during the Amarna period which witnessed major, but temporary, changes in Egyptian religion, the principles of building and decorating tombs, of mummification and of the provision of funerary furniture, remained unchanged. The strong belief in a second life probably reflected the regularity of the country's nature. The predictability of the sun rising every day after disappearing by night, the arrival of inundation water after the months of dryness and the sprouting of green shoots from the arid land may have given the inhabitants of the Nile valley the idea that, like the sun, the river and the plants, they will die but they will also live again. The connection between human life and the agricultural cycle is best seen in the Egyptian god of the dead, Osiris, who was also a god of vegetation and was frequently painted green.

To the Egyptian, his country was clearly divided into two main parts: Kemet, the black land, and Deshert, the red land or desert. The former is found in the Delta and along the Nile valley, while the latter is found on both east and west sides of the black land and occupies almost 96% of the total area of the country. Kemet and Deshert also symbolise life and death, not only because the former, unlike the latter, produced all the agricultural products of the country, but also because the Egyptian lived on the black land, while they buried their dead in the desert. Throughout the country numerous cemeteries are found in the desert at the edge of the cultivated land and in the cliffs bordering the inhabited areas.

INTRODUCTION

Tombs in the Nile valley are generally much better preserved, and therefore provide more information, than those in the Delta, of which little is known. This is also due primarily to the geographical features of the country. The Delta is alluvial and was thus much lower in ancient times, with far more marshlands. Today most of its ancient sites are covered by thick layers of silt deposit and are in addition densely populated, creating practical difficulties for excavations. On the other hand, tombs in Upper Egypt are cut into the cliffs, or constructed at the edge of the desert, at some distance from populated areas. Furthermore, the water table, the salinity and the humidity, all of which are destructive to the monuments, are far higher in the Delta than in Upper Egypt. The result is that the balance of our evidence for the study of various aspects of the Egyptian civilisation is heavily in favour of Upper Egypt and the Memphite region.

Thousands of tombs from various periods have been discovered, but undoubtedly many more remain under the sand. One might therefore ask how important are further excavations in various cemeteries? Would the information likely to be gained be repetitive? How much do we know of the Egyptian civilisation? The answers to these questions lie in the significance of the tomb to the ancient Egyptian. For as indicated this was not a mere burial place, but an eternal home for the deceased, where he dwells and also can be visited by contemporaries and by future generations. Evidence of such visits are clear in some tombs of the Teti cemetery at Saqqara for example, where guests left graffiti on the walls or scratched Senet-games on the floors presumably to entertain themselves for the duration of their visits. To impress these individuals, tomb decoration was not restricted to scenes of daily life, or those of the Hereafter in later tombs, but frequently included a perpetual record of the tomb owner's achievements on earth. These records constitute a major source of information for the historians in their attempt to reconstruct the history of ancient Egypt, as well as to study various aspects of Egyptian culture. Regarding history in its broadest terms as a big jigsaw puzzle, every tomb, every temple and indeed every artifact may help in gaining a more complete picture of this civilisation.

A superficial look at scenes in different tombs of a certain period can give the impression of repetitiveness, yet a careful examination of these scenes reveals enormous variations in details. The seeming similarities of scenes are due on the one hand to the fact that they are inspired by the same sources - the Egyptian nature and way of life - and are bound by the same social and artistic conventions of the period, and on the other hand to the lack of training for our eyes to discern the usually subtle differences in Egyptian scenes. Certainly the inhabitants of the Nile valley produced an art which is distinctly Egyptian, without abolishing the individuality of their artists, even though these remain in most cases anonymous. Each tomb therefore offers new information on the career of its owner and the administrative system, on the development of art and architecture, on the family structure and activities of daily life, while the preserved biographical inscriptions fill gaps in our knowledge of the situation and events of the time.

One of the main difficulties in dealing with Egyptian tombs is the lack of direct evidence for their dating. Because of the belief in eternal life, the ancient Egyptian did not feel the necessity to record the name of the king under whom he served, except occasionally to indicate his own role in an important event which took place in a specific reign, or to vaunt the fact that he received gifts, usually parts of his tomb - sarcophagus, false door, etc. from a particular king. Numerous tomb owners list among their titles priesthoods of certain kings. Yet such titles, while excluding a time before the reign of the mentioned monarch, do not automatically assign the tomb to a secure date, for the royal cult was maintained long after the death of any king. Studying individual, undated tombs is as baffling as seeing different episodes of a series, but with no coherent succession. However, much advance has been made in recent years in the study of the development of art and architecture of tombs of various periods and archaeologists can now rely on indirect evidence gained from stylistic and typological comparisons to date the tombs with a reasonable degree of precision.

From these tombs we are able to study various aspects of the life of the ancient Egyptians as well as their funerary beliefs and practices. For an understanding of these beliefs one is helped by a large body of funerary literature left by the Egyptians themselves. The first chapter of this book therefore draws on evidence from this literature and from the tombs. As there are considerable differences between the funerary practices of royalty, thought to be of divine essence, and private individuals, this book is devoted to the latter and accordingly relies for its sources on private tombs, which usually belonged to the official classes and which have in the past received less attention than that given to royal burials. Very little information

2

has survived on the lot of the lower classes in life or in death. For studying their lives we rely on information gained from settlements such as the one at Giza which belonged to the pyramid builders and the workmen's village at Deir el-Medina in Thebes. This is complemented by representations of the lower classes in tombs of the wealthier officials, although one might question the impartiality of such depictions. On the burials of the lower classes we are even less informed, but with more systematic excavations a clearer picture is emerging. A cemetery containing the burials of the workmen who built the pyramids, for example, has recently been excavated at Giza.

As tomb design changed through time, the second chapter of this book is reserved for the study of the main architectural features characteristic of the different periods of Egyptian history. Similarly, the nature and subject matter of the wall decoration varied from one period to another and the third chapter is accordingly devoted to the description of the various scenes expected in each period and to a discussion of their purposes.

One of the most curious facts is that almost all Egyptian tombs have been violated, hardly any escaped the attention of tomb robbers, and most were desecrated more than once. Experience must have taught the Egyptian that his tomb was vulnerable and with the valuable objects buried, it was too tempting for the lawless. Ancient texts record legal cases brought against tomb robbers who were convicted and punished. Yet the Egyptian continued his efforts to prepare the best house of eternity within his means and persisted with the burial of his most precious belongings with him. The logic behind such a resolution is difficult to understand. Did the Egyptian ignore the problem, of which he was almost certainly aware, and pretend that it did not exist, or did the tomb represent for him more than merely a place for the protection of his body and some valuables? Even if security was never guaranteed, tomb inscriptions indicate that the Egyptian expected his tomb to be the place where people would visit him, present him with offerings, remember him and mention his name, read about his earthly position and achievements and talk about him. The tomb was his monument on earth, and in that respect, if immortality was his main aspiration, he has certainly succeeded.

I: The House Of Death Is For Life

The mysteries of death and the Hereafter have always preoccupied the human mind, resulting in a wide variety of explanations and forming the basis of many religious beliefs. Like other peoples, the ancient Egyptians found it difficult to accept that life is only transitory and that death is inevitable; and as a result tried to overcome death by viewing it as the end of one form of existence and the beginning of another. While the first mode was totally earthly and limited in length, the latter was much more complex, full of uncertainties and dangers, but for those who had prepared for their afterlife and who had passed the necessary tests it was perpetual.

The preparation of a tomb was therefore the biggest 'investment' any Egyptian made during his lifetime. This applies, as far as we know, to the privileged class of officials who had the resources to build a tomb and who were fortunate enough to be granted a space for the tomb in one of the official cemeteries in the capital or the provinces. Our information on the poorer classes, which no doubt formed the bulk of the population, is very limited and mostly gained from their representations in the tombs of the upper classes, representations which therefore may or may not be entirely objective and certainly do not deal with their afterlife.

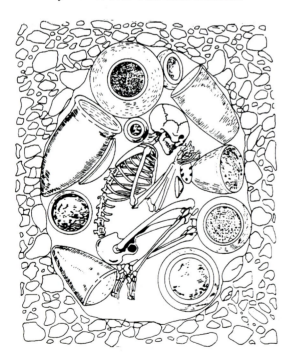

Fig. 1 Predynastic burial from El-Amra

From the Predynastic period, evidence exists of a belief in the Hereafter: graves were lined with mud,

mud-brick or wood and food, clothing, ornaments, protective amulets, figurines and objects of daily use were buried with the deceased. The body was also mostly placed in a contracted, foetal position, ready for rebirth (fig. 1). With the historic era and the introduction of writing the Egyptian became better able to record his beliefs and aspirations in an unambiguous manner. From the Old Kingdom onwards the literature emphasises the importance of building and decorating a tomb. Thus Prince Hardjedef, probably from the Fifth Dynasty, advises his son saying: 'Furnish your house in the graveyard and enrich your place in the west. Given that death humbles us, given that life exalts us, the house of death is for life'. Similar advice is repeatedly met in Egyptian wisdom literature of all periods, as for example in the instruction to King Merikare of the First Intermediate Period. From the New Kingdom, the wise Any echoes the same ideas by writing: 'Furnish your place in the valley, the grave that shall hide your corpse. Make it a worthy target for you, emulate the great departed, who now rest within their tombs'.

The wise Any also tells his son of the need for one to be ready and 'not to say "I am young to be taken"', for when death comes he steals away the infant who is in his mother's lap, like him who reaches old age'. Many other texts also stress the fact that death does not discriminate between the famous and the obscure nor between the young and old. Ankhsheshonq, from the Late Period says: 'Do not delay to get yourself a tomb on the mountain; you do not know the length of your life'. While such advice is valid at all times and places, it was particularly relevant for the ancient Egyptians because of their relatively short life span. The high rate of infant mortality resulted in the average life expectancy being very low, and as a result of the apparently too frequent death in childbirth, this average was lower among women than men. In excavations conducted by the author in the Teti cemetery at Saqqara during 1995-96, the human remains of 106 individuals were uncovered. Of these, 30 were males, 33 females, it was impossible to identify the sex of 30 and 13 were mostly infants too badly preserved to include in the study. Of the 93 studied cases 17.2% were children aged between 1 and 11, and 9.67% were sub-adults aged 12-17 years. The combined total of individuals 17 years and under was 26.88%, and had it been possible to include the 13 unstudied remains, this percentage would have been much higher. We also have to bear in mind that infant bones do not preserve as well as those of adults and that infants were sometimes buried in the settlement rather than in the necropolis. Reports of infant burials under the floors of houses are known from the settlement site in Abydos during the First Intermediate Period. In our sample at Saqqara only 13.9% appear to have lived beyond 46 years, which is a normal mortality pattern in the ancient world. In the age group of 18-25 there were 3 males, 11 females and 1 unidentified. Women were frequently accompanied by the skeletal remains of a child or a foetus, buried immediately next to them, or even sometimes inside the same wooden coffin. The sample is of course too small to give a general pattern, but the figures seem to conform with others obtained from different sites.

Almost all the above-mentioned individuals from the Teti cemetery are dated to the latter part of the Eighteenth Dynasty; they also belong to the lower echelon of the bureaucracy as may be gathered from the number of the scarab seals found with them. Although their bodies were not mummified, these were wrapped with linen bandages and either placed directly in the sand, or wrapped in reed mats, or less frequently placed in coffins, often of anthropoid shape and generally made of poor quality local wood and thus badly preserved. These burials were sometimes accompanied by a limited amount of funerary equipment - one or two, rarely more, pottery jars, faience amulets and rings, small alabaster vessels presumably for cosmetics, beads which originally formed necklaces and collars, kohl tubes made of ivory or glass, and very rarely small gold objects, like earrings and amulets, etc. One of the best equipped burials was that of a woman and a child/foetus, placed together in a rectangular wooden coffin with arched top. Having died very young and presumably in childbirth, the woman was accompanied by some objects of toilet and religious figurines related to fertility and birth. These were put in two baskets, deposited outside the coffin near the head end and included the following: a pottery juglet with an applied handle which is probably a perfume container, a palm-column kohl flask made of translucent dark blue glass decorated with medium blue, opaque white and yellow trails, a kohl stick of blue glass, and a small alabaster jar. Near the baskets were 25 faience amulets with thread holes, of various shapes - fly, moondisc and crescent, Taweret, Bes, fish and pomegranate, together with two pottery figures of cobras which may be a form of the goddess Renenutet who represents the concept of nursing or raising children, a wooden headrest and a pottery figurine of a naked girl lying on a pottery bed, probably intended to

Pl. 1 Objects accompanying the burial of a woman and a child, Saqqara, Dynasty 18

ensure fertility and birth in life and in death (pl. 1).

These burials represent a very important source of information about the Egyptian population and their funerary beliefs. The possible common knowledge, at least to contemporaries, that they contained no riches of significant importance, made them unattractive to ancient tomb robbers and accordingly resulted in their survival almost intact. However, in the quest for spectacular mastaba-tombs constructed on the bed-rock, usually located below the above-mentioned burials, little attention was paid by archaeologists to the full recording of these burials until relatively recently. As a consequence, a great deal of evidence was permanently lost to us on the beliefs and customs of this class of society. Such a loss is even more regrettable when we consider our lack of knowledge on the still lower classes of society, the peasants and labourers.

The upper and middle echelons of the bureaucracy formed more privileged classes, much richer than the rest of the population and apparently also closer to the palace. Even the children of the provincial administrators appear to have spent a period of 'education' and frequently employment in the capital, perhaps at or near the palace, before succeeding to their fathers' responsibilities. Rather than being buried in the sand in what appears to be unmarked graves, these individuals owned tombs in one of the official cemeteries.

The type of tomb depended on its location. In the Memphite cemeteries - Giza, Saqqara, Abusir, etc. - where the edges of the cultivated area were formed of plateaux, most tombs had to be constructed either of mud-brick or of stone depending on the means of the owner (pl. 2). Stone no doubt fitted better with the Egyptian aspiration for eternity and was accordingly preferred. But the quality of the stone also varied according to its strength, density and suitability for relief cutting. Some of the best stones for such purposes were the limestone of Tura on the east bank of the river opposite Memphis and the red granite of Aswan. But these were royal quarries, although certain individuals received some pieces from them as a special favour from the king. Little is known from the cemeteries in the Delta, but the evidence shows that tombs there were not dissimilar from those in the Memphite region. In Upper Egypt - including El-Hawawish, El-Hagarsa, Thebes and Aswan - where the fertile valley is bordered on both east and west sides by mountain ridges, tombs were excavated into the mountain slope (pl. 3). As the quality of the rock varied from one area to the other

and was not predictable, even inside the different parts of the same tomb, the decoration of many of these rock-cut tombs could not be executed in relief but was rather painted on mud or gypsum plaster.

Although the size and lavishness of a tomb no doubt reflect the importance of its occupant, as a status symbol, individuals were probably not free to decide on the size or the location of their tombs. The cemeteries, the 'cities of eternity' belonged to the king and were highly organised, with administrative personnel responsible for their management. The king granted officials specific areas of land in the cemetery for the building of their tombs, each according to his/her position. The area allocated to each category of officials varied from time to time depending on the economic and political conditions of the country and perhaps on the level of support the king required from them. The royal control of the cemeteries appears in the unambiguous statements of Iri/Tetiseneb of the Teti cemetery at Saqqara who says: 'As for this tomb which I made in the necropolis, it was the king who granted its place for me, as one who is honoured before the king, one who does what his lord favours'. Describing his funeral, Amenemhat of the New Kingdom also says that he was 'interred into land given by the king, into the tomb of the west'. Close to Iri/Tetiseneb's tomb at Saqqara is another tomb which originally belonged to a vizier named Hesi whose name and figures have been chiselled out, presumably as a punishment for a crime of some sort. The tomb was then reallocated to a man named Seshemnefer, who also claimed that the tomb was given to him as a boon from the king. Such direct references to the king's donation of land are, however, omitted in the vast majority of biographical and tomb inscriptions. Yet if a burial ground could only be obtained through the favours of the king, at least in the official cemeteries, there was perhaps no need for tomb owners to state the obvious. On the other hand the role of the king in providing for the Hereafter of his officials is regularly acknowledged by them in a formula written in practically each tomb, with slight variation:

> An offering which the king gives and/to Anubis, who is on his hill, who is in the embalming place, lord of the sacred land (gives); that he be buried well in the western desert, in his tomb of the necropolis (title and name of the tomb owner).

Pl. 2 (top) Mastaba tombs in the Teti cemetery at Saqqara
Pl. 3 (bottom) Rock-cut tombs at El-Hagarsa

Variations to this formula may replace Anubis by Osiris, and may wish the deceased different things - that offerings come forth for him at certain feasts, that he may travel upon the beautiful roads of the west in peace, that he be accompanied by his Ka, etc. (fig. 2). The mention of Anubis and Osiris in the formulae is understandable; Anubis was the god of mummification, thus responsible for the preservation of the body and was also regarded as the lord of the necropolis. Osiris, who was murdered and cut into pieces by his brother Seth, has, with the help of his sister/wife Isis and the god Anubis, conquered death. He was resurrected and became the god of the dead. Yet the nature of the 'offering which the king gives', regularly written at the head of the formulae, is not entirely clear. It may refer, at least in its origin, to an offering made to Anubis and Osiris so that they may help the deceased, or to offerings directly made to the deceased. But it is equally possible that it at least included the donation of the land which each individual buried in these cemeteries should have received.

Weni was particularly close. Equally, Djau of Deir el-Gebrawi in Upper Egypt boasts of the fact that he received similar pieces for his tomb from King Pepy II.

On the other hand, numerous inscriptions were left by tomb owners stating the fact that they paid the men who worked for them. Mehi/Mehnes of Saqqara says:'I made payments to the stonemasons so that they were satisfied', Meruka of Giza also says: 'as for all the artisans who made this work for me, I made them praise god for the reward which I have given them', and Remenuka/Imi even lists the rewards he paid, stating: 'I made this tomb in exchange for bread and beer which I gave to all the artisans who made this tomb. Behold, I have certainly given them very great wages out of all the linen which they asked for and they thanked god for it'.

While the area of the land on which the tomb was built was granted by the king and reflected the owner's position in the hierarchy of the administration, the lavishness of the tomb reflected the individual's personal means. The two aspects do

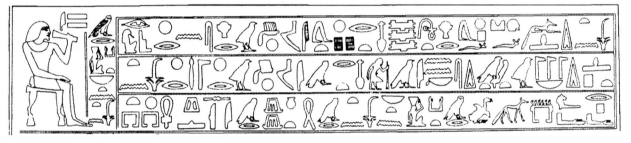

Fig. 2 The offering formula, Neferseshemre/Sheshi, Saqqara, Dynasty 6

The above-mentioned case of Seshemnefer of Saqqara was unusual, for he received a complete tomb, although it was no doubt common knowledge among his contemporaries that it was formerly owned by a disgraced person. A similar case is also found in the Unis cemetery where a royal princess, Idut, was given the tomb of the vizier Ihy, after all inscriptions had been adapted for her use. In all such cases a careful examination usually reveals the identity of the original owner. Debehni and Merkhufu of Giza, on the other hand, had the cost of constructing their own tombs totally provided by King Menkaure of Dynasty 4. These were exceptional cases, for it was customary for the tomb owners to meet the cost of building their tombs. Occasionally, favourite officials were presented with certain elements of their tombs as a special honour from the king. Thus Weni received two entrance jambs, a false door, an offering slab and a sarcophagus cut from the limestone quarry of Tura as a gift from King Pepy I of Dynasty 6, to whom

not always correspond; private property and family size and responsibilities played significant roles in determining what portion of an individual's income, all in kind, could be spent on the building and the decoration of his tomb. Accordingly, some of the larger tombs are cheaply constructed with mud-brick, while other smaller ones used good quality stone and were fully decorated. The nature of decoration no doubt also affected the cost of preparing a tomb. Different types of reliefs required different skills and some were more time consuming than others; raised relief was probably more costly than the incised. While colour enhanced the appearance of the relief and increased its value, the painted scenes on plaster were presumably the least expensive since they involved no carving. Finally, a distinguished sculptor or painter must have been paid more than a less able one, and an examination of tomb decoration of any period clearly shows varying standards between tombs, ranging from outstanding to mediocre.

The lack of means to build an adequate tomb may be gathered from an interesting statement by Iri/Tetiseneb who built a mud-brick mastaba at Saqqara and wrote: 'I did the work in it (the tomb) with my own hands, together with my children and brothers'. The connection between the tomb and an individual's means appears also in the inscriptions of Djau of Deir el-Gebrawi, who buried his father with him in one tomb. In his biography he emphasises the fact that this action was out of his love for his father, the desire to be with him in one place and to see him every day, and 'not indeed because of the lack of wealth for making a second tomb' (fig. 3). Regardless of the degree of truth in Djau's claim and without doubting his filial affection, one can see that the tomb was not considered by the Egyptians as simply a burial place, but also as a status symbol and an indication of means, and it was this lack of means that Djau was so concerned to deny before his contemporaries.

When and Where the Tomb was built

The time which the construction and decoration of the tomb required depended on its size, complexity and lavishness, as well as the means available to its owner. The work included the excavation of the subterranean shafts and burial chambers, the cutting of stone or the manufacturing of mud-bricks to be used in the building of the superstructure, which included the exterior walls of the mastaba as well as the interior rooms of the chapel. In rock-cut tombs, the whole tomb - chapel as well as burial apartments - were of course excavated into the native rock of a hill. The work also involved the preparation of the wall surfaces for receiving scenes and inscriptions; stone or rock surfaces were smoothed and plaster was applied wherever it was necessary to hide defects or to provide a flat surface over bad quality rock.

The final stage was the decoration of these walls in painting, relief, or painted relief. Sendjemib/Mehi of Giza, proudly recorded the fact that he completed the tomb of his father 'in one year and [two-thirds] while he was still in the embalming place for the treatment of his mummy'. But this was not an ordinary case; not only was Sendjemib/Inti, father of Sendjemib/Mehi, a vizier, but he appears to have been particularly close to King Djedkare of Dynasty 5. He received, and was allowed to inscribe in his tomb, two letters from Djedkare, one of which was said to be in the king's own handwriting. The generosity of the king in providing for the funerary expenses of one of his favoured officials is emphasised in the inscriptions of the tomb. The son was also a high administrator and was destined, although somewhat later, to succeed his father in the vizierate. Finally, there was a special need for swiftness since the man died before his burial place was prepared. Despite all this, the period of twenty months during which the tomb was made, must have seemed unusually short

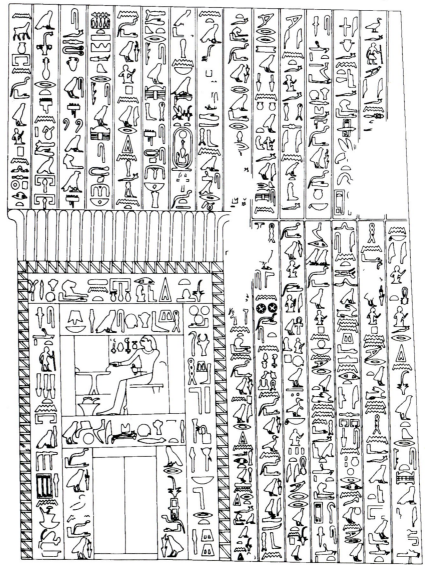

Fig. 3 Biographical inscription, Djau, Deir el-Gebrawi, Dynasty 6

9

Pl. 4 False door, Kaaper, Saqqara, Dynasty 6

to the son for him to consider it worthy of being recorded for his contemporaries and the future generations. We may assume therefore that this was not the norm and that the preparation of a tomb must have stretched over a number of years. In the New Kingdom, an ostracon dates the beginning of work on Senenmut's Theban tomb to Year 7, while a payroll ostracon indicates work was continuing in Year 16, 9 years later.

Officials presumably supervised the construction of their tombs which were usually located in the cemetery of the town where they held office not where they were born, although the two were not necessarily different. Thus at periods of centralised government, almost all officials had their tombs in the cemeteries of the capital, preferably in the proximity of the pyramid or the tomb of the king they served. While at times of decentralisation, most officials were buried in the provinces. Such changes, however, do not appear to have been orchestrated or even desired by the officials themselves, but were, rather, planned by the central government for different administrative or economic objectives. Building a tomb in the vicinity of the king's pyramid on the other hand, did not seem to

grant its owner automatic access to the Hereafter, otherwise the powerful provincial administrators would have resisted the decentralisation reforms. Admission to a perpetual life was subject to complex requirements (see below) and was not influenced by tomb location. Individuals buried near a king were either simply in the personal service of that king, or, for later generations, were allowed to be buried near earlier members of their families. The evidence does not support the often repeated statement that the fortunes of the officials in the afterlife depended on the king's need for them and his permission to build their resting places in the vicinity of his; nor does it seem true that the depiction of a workman in an official's tomb secured him a place in the Hereafter.

It was more practical and therefore the norm to construct the tomb where the official held office and where his family resided and his sons were expected to succeed him. It also had the advantage to the tomb owner of being buried where he was best known, for according to Egyptian wisdom literature 'The godly man who is far from his town, his worth is not better known than that of another. He who dies far from his town is buried out of pity'. Considering the belief in the continuing reliance of the dead on the living and the need for remembrance and for a constant supply of offerings, the presence near the descendants was of great importance. Each town had its cemetery, usually in the nearest suitable plateau or cliff at the edge of the cultivated land. As towns existed equally on the east and west banks of the Nile, so did the cemeteries, despite the connection between the west where the sun sets and the realm of the dead or the western desert and the necropolis. Yet due to an innate conservatism, standard formulae referring to the burial in the western desert was used by individuals buried in the east. Thus Tjeti-iker, a governor of Akhmim in Upper Egypt at the end of Dynasty 6, who was buried in the eastern cliff of El-Hawawish wrote in his tomb: 'An offering which the king gives and Anubis, who is in the embalming place, lord of the sacred land (gives), that he may be buried in his tomb of the necropolis in the western desert'. While the choice of the eastern as against the western hills as a necropolis was dictated by the location of the town itself, the Egyptians designed tombs so that the false door, an important architectural element in the tomb, was positioned in the west wall of the offering room in the tomb chapel (fig. 3, pl. 4). Thus every time the deceased's Ka descended to the burial chamber to be united with its body after receiving offerings in the chapel, it was actually going west.

Longevity

We are never told at what age the Egyptian started the construction of his tomb. But it should be stated from the outset that the evidence suggests that unlike the people with modest means (see above), the upper classes, including the king and the higher officials, seem to have enjoyed on average a relatively long life span. This was no doubt the result of better nutrition and medical care. Thus King Pepy II of Dynasty 6 is said to have ruled for over ninety years (although the actual figure is disputed) and King Ramesses II was on the throne for sixty-seven years. Some officials also had long careers. Netjeruhotep, for example, claimed that at seventy-three he led an expedition to the alabaster quarries of Hatnub. Many priests recorded unusually long lives or careers. Bakenkhons from the reign of Ramesses II wrote a summary of his life at the age of eighty-five, and Nebnetjeru of Dynasty 22 was still healthy at ninety-six, while Besmut of Dynasty 26 even reached the age of ninety-nine. The centenarian Pepyankh-heryib of Dynasty 6 left an inscription in his tomb at Meir stating that he was already a hundred years old. One hundred years was the ideal limit of earthly existence, although occasionally ten or even twenty additional years were expressed as a wish. During these extra years the individual was supposed to reach the pinnacle of wisdom and purity and be better prepared for the afterlife. The Coffin Texts from the Middle Kingdom state that 'Each person familiar with this text will complete 110 years of life, of which 10 years will be outside his inadequacy and his impurity, outside his offences and his insincerity, as in the case of a man who was unknowing and became knowing'.

The above-mentioned examples of long earthly life were certainly the exception rather than the rule, so unusual that they were judged worthy of inscribing for posterity, but none found it of interest to record when they started to build their tomb. On the other hand, an examination of tomb inscriptions shows that the greater majority of these were written after their owners had attained the peak of their career, since the titles recorded on all walls were their highest ones, without evidence of alterations or later additions. Only rarely are we able to detect a promotion of an individual during or after the construction of his tomb. Seshemnefer is an example of those who were promoted after the majority of their tomb's decoration was completed. Only on the pillars and architrave of the portico in front of the entrance of his Giza tomb, are the high titles of judge and vizier recorded. Instances are also

Fig. 4 Stela of Atjetka, El-Hawawish, Dynasty 6

Pl. 5 Stela of Iret, El-Hawawish, Dynasty 6

known of men who reached the top of the ladder in the administration hierarchy, yet died unexpectedly before the work on their tombs even began. Sendjemib/Inti, a vizier under Djedkare of Dynasty 5 and Djau, a governor of the two provinces of Abydos and Deir el-Gebrawi under Pepy II, had their tombs prepared for them by their eldest sons after their death. The precise age of either Sendjemib/Inti or Djau when they attained their distinguished posts is not known. Yet one would expect the vizierate, the highest administrative office in the land, to be placed in the hand of an experienced, mature-aged man, even though family connections as well as close relationship with the palace seem to have influenced the choice in general. With regard to Djau, not only was he a governor of two provinces but also his similarly named son was old enough to be associated with him in governing the provinces during his lifetime and to succeed him in all his duties after his death. Both Sendjemib/Inti and Djau were of age, yet neither of them had his tomb ready.

Studies of the biographies of some officials are also useful in determining the approximate age of their owners when they built their resting places. Weni, for example, was a young man under Teti of Dynasty 6. He then served Pepy I in a number of capacities before he was appointed by Merenre as governor of Upper Egypt, residing at Abydos where he built his tomb. From the Eighteenth Dynasty, Ineny successively served under Amenhotep I, Thutmose I, Thutmose II and Thutmose III together with Hatshepsut, when he probably prepared his burial place. These examples lead us to the same conclusion: that the Egyptian officials constructed their eternal resting places rather late in their life; a broad age of forty to fifty seems to agree in general with the evidence. Perhaps it was only then that the individual was granted a piece of land in the cemetery in recognition of his services or his age, before which he was presumably buried in a separate shaft in or around the tomb of an earlier member of his family. Presumably such a restriction did not apply to members of the royal family.

The evidence from human remains in some tombs seems to support the approximate age of forty to fifty for the commencement of tomb building. The unfortunate owner of mastaba Giza 2140 completed the construction of his tomb and started its decoration, but did not progress beyond the recording of a few titles in only one line of inscription which stopped short of writing his name. One may assume that the owner died not long after he began the preparation of his resting place. An examination of his skeletal remains revealed that he was approximately fifty years old. Another interesting case is that of Nedjetempet, mother of Mereruka, a vizier of Teti who was buried in front of Teti's pyramid at Saqqara. She was probably the wife of Meruka of Giza. Nedjetempet was not buried in a shaft in her husband's tomb as was common, nor in a shaft in her son's tomb, but rather she owned an independent tomb not far from that of her son at Saqqara. The examination of her skeletal remains again indicated that she was over fifty years of age at death.

Tombs Completed after the Death of the Owner

With the construction of the tomb starting late in one's life and extending over a relatively long period, it is not surprising to find that a large number of tombs were left in various stages of completion. In some instances the work was finished by a member of the deceased's immediate family, mostly a son, or even by a friend. Thus, at El-Hawawish in Upper Egypt for example, the tomb of Tjeti-iker was completed by his son Kheni, while that of Ti was made or completed by his daughter Nefertjentet and his brother Tjeri, who left inscriptions commemorating their praiseworthy deeds. Tomb owners who died before commencing the decoration of their tombs were frequently provided with a tomb stela, a kind of gravestone, which was placed at the entrance to the shaft leading to the burial chamber. The majority of stelae depicted the owner seated at an offering table and detailed his names and titles. These stelae were presumably considered as a substitute for wall decoration since the offering table scene was one of the commonest representations in chapels and also regularly appeared on panels of false doors. Occasionally the scenes of the stelae were expanded to include other members of the deceased's family, wife or children, or to show simple scenes, like the slaughtering of a sacrificial animal, the milking of a cow, or the like (pl. 5).

Stelae were usually presented by a member of the family, thus the stela of Atjetka was made by her son Mery, and that of Henut also by her son Hengi, while that of Tjetuti was made for her by her husband Sebebi, all from El-Hawawish (fig. 4).

Such charitable acts by the relatives were probably done out of love for the departed ones, but perhaps also in the hope that they would be treated similarly in the future. After building an entire tomb for his father, Sendjemib/Mehi left a reminder to his own son by referring to himself as one 'whose son shall do the like for him'. But burying the dead, whether related or unrelated, was considered a virtue on par with upholding justice, raising orphans and protecting widows, for example. Thus Horemkhuf of the Middle Kingdom boasted of the fact that he organised his parents' burials: 'I looked after the house of those who had raised me, they are buried and made to live'. A more common claim however was that which Neferseshemre of Dynasty 6 wrote: 'I buried the one who had no son'. Despite possibly the best intentions a huge number of tombs were left incomplete or even devoid of any inscriptions including the owner's name. This feature, however, was less prevalent in the cemeteries of the capital than those of the provinces, where the long distances from the main towns and in most cases the excessive height of the mountains on which the cemeteries are located, made them less accessible and perhaps more susceptible to neglect. Out of 884 tombs cut into the mountain of El-Hawawish, the cemetery of Akhmim in Upper Egypt, 60 tombs had their walls plastered and decorated, with none of the others showing evidence of ever being inscribed. It is true that a number of these tombs were provided with tomb stelae, some of which were found in the cemetery. Nevertheless, the vast majority of tombs on this 330 metre high mountain must have been left totally undecorated.

Such a failure to decorate tombs simply appears to defeat the very purpose of the tomb. The full and explicit identification of the owner, in figure, titles and names, was essential for the deceased's Ka to recognise its resting place and accordingly its body. An irony of fate may be found in mastaba Giza 2140 where, as previously mentioned, the unfortunate owner recorded his titles in the only line of inscriptions in his tomb but for some reason stopped short of writing his name, thus the tomb remains anonymous.

Owning any tomb, large or small, decorated or undecorated was, however, a favour reserved for the royal family and the administrative classes, for we know almost nothing about the fate of the populace, the larger portion of society. Perhaps they were buried in unmarked graves in the nearest desert. We are, moreover, uncertain whether the often repeated claim by the privileged classes that they buried 'he who had no son' applied also to the populace or was restricted to people of their own standing.

VULNERABILITY AND STRENGTH

The wealthy Egyptian built a tomb and endowed a piece of land, or had it allocated to him by the king, to produce income in order to provide for his funerary services, which were maintained by one or more funerary priests. In his instructions to his son Hardjedef says:

> Choose for him (i.e., the funerary priest) a plot among your fields, well-watered every year. He profits you more than your own son. Prefer him even to your heir.

Despite this, if a will was left organising the use of the land and the role of each priest, it was the eldest son who was usually appointed as executor of the will, often with the proviso that if he let his father's services be neglected, he would not be entitled to any of his property. Kaemnefert of Giza from Dynasty 5, represented himself with his son standing in front of him with the words of his will (fig. 5). They are both before 15 witnesses who are all named. Such arrangements inscribed in tombs must also have been kept in an official record. The sources indicate the presence of some officials with titles directly related to these responsibilities in the administration of the cemeteries and in the keeping of their records. Whether the son carried out his duties or not, certainly the funerary services were not maintained perpetually. Tombs appear to have been neglected and were allowed to fall into ruins, perhaps after a few generations, although the restoration of the ancestors' tombs remained always a virtue claimed by some, as for example Khnumhotep of Beni Hasan who says:

> I made to live the name of my fathers which I found obliterated upon the doorways, learned in the signs, exact in reading, without placing one sign in the place of another. Behold a good son, making to flourish the names of the ancestors, is Nehera's son Khnumhotep, justified, possessor of veneration.

Fig. 5 Funerary will, Kaemnefert, Giza, Dynasty 5

In addition to the inevitable neglect of the tomb with time, there was the ever present threat of theft. The protection of a man's resting place after he died was a worry to the ancient Egyptian and men were appointed to guard the property of the dead. Yet the country experienced periods of relative anarchy, internal wars, or severe famines, as for example during the First Intermediate Period when death apparently spread throughout the land. From this period we read in the inscriptions of Merer of Edfu: 'I buried the dead and nourished the living, wherever I went in this drought which had occurred'. Ironically, from the same period the sage Ipuwer lamented the situation saying:

> There is blood everywhere, no shortage of dead. Behold, many dead are buried in the river. The stream is the grave and the tomb became the stream.

It was also then that most tombs, at least those belonging to the nobles and the bureaucracy, were desecrated. Describing this sad state of affairs Ipuwer says:

> He who could not make a coffin owns a tomb. See, those who owned tombs are cast on high ground. He who could not make a grave owns a treasury.

That these burials contained riches was no doubt known to the common people, and accordingly at a time of desperate need, coupled perhaps with instability and lack of security and order, such places became vulnerable targets for the lawless. But tomb robbery was not restricted to times of anarchy, it was presumably practised in all periods, with our best documented cases coming from the New Kingdom. A body of court proceedings from the Twentieth Dynasty gives a detailed description of the activities of a gang of thieves robbing tombs, mostly private ones but also some belonging to the royal family, on the west bank of Thebes. The collection of papyri documenting the investigation reveals some astonishing information; the men were arrested, interrogated, confessed to their crimes although after physical punishment, everything being recorded in detail. The papyri provides the names of the thieves, the tombs robbed, the methods used to enter the tombs, records of items stolen and damage inflicted on bodies and coffins, and penalties exacted in such cases, which amounted to the mutilation of the nose and ears or even death. Many members of the gang proved to be artisans, who may have been employed in the necropolis, hence their knowledge of how to gain entry with minimum effort through tunnelling from one tomb to the other by the shortest possible route.

So frequent were the robberies that they necessitated the removal of some royal mummies from their individual tombs and placement in a single cache, unmarked and with no tempting funerary furnishings. The following is an extract from the confession of a gang of thieves:

> We went to rob from the tombs in accordance with the practice in which we were regularly engaged. We found that the pyramid of King Sobekemsaf differed from the pyramids and tombs we usually went to rob. We .... tunnelled into this pyramid of this king through its back ... We took lighted torches in our hands and went down. We cleared the rubble we found at the entrance of its recess and found this god lying at the rear ... We also found the burial place of Queen Nebkhaas, his queen ... We cleared this and discovered her ... We

opened their sarcophagi and their coffins in which they lay, and found this mummy of this king equipped with a sword, a great quantity of amulets and of golden jewellery on his neck, and his headpiece of gold upon him. The noble mummy of this king was completely covered with gold, and his coffin overlaid with gold and silver inside and out, and decorated with every sort of precious stone. We collected the gold we found on this mummy of this god along with his amulets and jewels which were at his neck and the coffin in which he lay. We found the queen and we collected all that we found on her likewise. We set fire to their coffins (after) we took away their furnishings which we found with them, objects of gold, silver and bronze, and divided them among ourselves, so that 20 deben of gold was the share of each of the eight of us, resulting in 160 deben. We ferried back across to Thebes.

Despite such a confession one of the offenders managed to secure his release through bribery, resuming his robbing activities only to be arrested again three years later. Corruption must have been rife at certain times, and a papyrus from the reign of Ramesses IX contains a long list of thieves who had stolen metal, mainly bronze, from royal tombs. The list includes scribes, merchants, temple watchmen, etc.

These activities of stealing the deceased's possessions were neither restricted to Thebes nor to the Ramesside Period. An examination of the tombs in the Teti cemetery at Saqqara shows that the practice started much earlier. The robbers' tunnels linking a number of tombs are frequently so direct and precise that one is inclined to think that only men with exact knowledge of the subterranean layout of all these tombs could have been so successful in cutting them. This may suggest that many tombs were robbed shortly after the interment took place, and perhaps was done by some of the men who constructed the tomb. Thus, even during the stable and secure period at the height of the Old Kingdom and despite the presence of guards in the necropolis, the Egyptian did not seem to have much confidence in the system; perhaps enough had already happened by then to shake his trust. Yet the Egyptian did not stop building tombs and placing riches in them. There was little that he could do

other than leave an inscription in a prominent place in his tomb where he enumerated his past deeds and virtues while still on earth as well as his present powers in the Hereafter, then appeal to the living for help, and finally threaten any violator of his tomb with revenge in the Netherworld. So Ankhmahor, Khentika and Inumin, all viziers buried in the Teti cemetery, remind the living on earth that they exercised justice and never used force against any man because they wanted their name to be good before the god and their reputation to be good before all men. Khentika also claims to have rescued the wretched, to have given bread to the hungry and clothing to the naked and to have brought the stranded to land and buried him who had no son, and he affirms that he never said any evil thing against any man. Furthermore, he feared his father and was gracious to his mother and brought up their children properly, etc. Khentika then warns anyone against entering his tomb before first purifying himself, and threatens any violator to enter into judgement with him in the west. Also he says he will personally seize his neck like a bird and cast fear into him, so that he becomes an example to those living who are upon earth. Likewise, Khentika promises those who enter his tomb, after purifying themselves, and presenting offerings to him, that he will be their supporter in the necropolis and will not allow anything they hate to happen to them, since he knows everything that an excellent spirit knows. The request to enter the tomb in a state of purity without eating something that a spirit detests is repeated by many tomb owners. Hesi, a near contemporary of Khentika, makes a similar request, but curiously adds a prohibition against anyone who had copulated with women, from entering his tomb (fig. 6). Ankhmahor wishes his descendants and his predecessors well, and warns them saying: `Anything which you may do against this tomb of the necropolis the like will be done against your property (i.e., tomb)'. He also threatens 'I will seize his neck like a bird, when the fear of me is cast in him, so that the spirits (akhu) and those who are upon earth may see it and may fear an excellent spirit'.

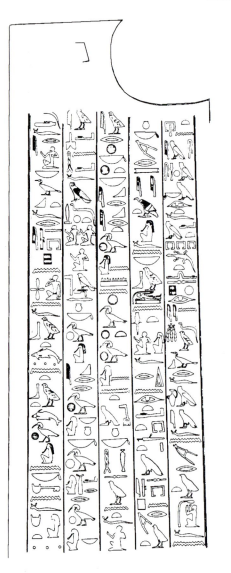

Fig. 6 Request for purity, Hesi, Saqqara, Dynasty 6

Letters to the Dead

These inscriptions suggest that the dead possessed great powers that could influence not only the lot of the dead, but equally the lot of the living; a picture supported also by the evidence gained from a group of documents usually called 'Letters to the Dead' (fig. 7). This literary genre with stereotyped phrases represents letters written in hieratic, mostly on pottery bowls, but sometimes on a papyrus or a strip of linen and left in tombs, possibly on offering tables, for the deceased to receive together with the food and drink they required. Since the dead were able to travel in and out the tomb, sometimes very far in the sky or in the Netherworld, letters were a logical means of communication, in the same way as the living communicated with each other and as the dead were in a sense always present. These letters, however, were not simply aimed at remaining in contact with the beloved departed, but had practical purposes, always calling on the dead, with the power they possess, to intervene on the writers' behalf in earthly matters. Thus one letter represents an appeal to the deceased to arise and to waken his father, brothers and friends so that they may take vengeance on the offender. In another letter a widower addresses his dead wife after he had suffered some misfortunes, perhaps financial. He entertained three possibilities: first, he wondered if she was aware of what had happened to him and reminded her that her children were suffering as well; second, he considered the possibility that the harm was done against her will and suggests that she should enlist the help of her powerful father also in the Netherworld; third, he questioned if she was still nursing some grievance against him and asked her to forget it for the children's sake, also to forgive as one would wish for forgiveness. Another widower was certain that his problems emanated from his departed wife and therefore he wrote to her three years after her death:

> What evil thing have I done to you that I should have come into this wretched state in which I am? ... since I lived with you as husband down to this day, what have I done to you that I must hide?

He then reminded her that when she became ill he brought her a master-physician and that when she died he spent 'eight months without eating or drinking like a man' and that he 'wept exceedingly' and had no relationship with other women, but 'you do not know good from bad'.

The intervention sought from a dead relative was not only against human acts of malice, but in one instance this was against a disease. According to Egyptian beliefs many illnesses were caused by evil dead spirits and were usually treated by magical incantations, but a letter to a dead person could achieve the same result. The following is a letter from a widow named Dedi to her dead husband the priest Intef blaming him for failing to look after their ill maid-servant.

> Given by Dedi to the priest Intef, born of Iunakht. As for this maid-servant Imiu who is sick, you do not fight for her night and day with every man who is doing harm to her and every woman who is doing harm to her ... Fight for her! Watch over her! Save her from all men and women who are doing harm to her! Then shall your house and your children be established. May you listen well.

The number of these letters suggests a widespread custom and obviously a strong belief in the power of the dead to influence events of the living. Among the wishes written in some Theban tombs of Dynasty 18 one reads: 'May he behold his house of the living, so as to make protection for his children every day and for ever and ever'. Such a wish suggests that the dead father could be present in his family home providing protection for his children. Letters ask a dead person to bring a lawsuit, no doubt before the gods of the Hereafter, against the offending party. One letter urges a mother to arbitrate between her two sons, the one living, the other dead. The evidence suggests therefore that the mere fact of death made little difference to the individual powers or rights.

Despite the addresses to the living - appeals, promises and threats - written in tombs, and despite the fear of the power of the dead, almost all tombs were violated at one time or another, perhaps even more than once. Ironically, those who could read these inscriptions were limited to the official classes, the populace being illiterate. In fact it is uncertain whether all members of the family of an official could also read and write. The letters to the dead, for example, demonstrate such a fixed mode of composition that they were most probably produced by professional letter-writers. The security of tombs was certainly not mainly under threat by the educated classes, and therefore all the written threats appear to be worthless and were simply not heeded. It is obvious that the tomb robbers themselves had no fear of the dead. It is extremely rare now for archaeologists to find undisturbed tombs, and these are usually those which were too poor to deserve the efforts and risks of robbing them. Only contemporaries and particularly the necropolis workers and guards could have had knowledge of the contents of various tombs, and the latter's involvement was imperative since the operation of emptying shafts leading to the burial chambers required time and secrecy.

At El-Hawawish, the cemetery of Akhmim on the east bank, of the 884 tombs cut into the mountain only two were discovered intact, yet both were extremely poor. Formed of a shallow shaft leading to a very small burial chamber, each tomb contained

Fig. 7 Letter to the dead

an uninscribed, roughly made wooden coffin and unmummified human remains, with no funerary belongings, although one was accompanied by two pleated dresses inside the coffin. These were presumably loyal servants of the governors of the province and were buried in the vicinity of their rich tombs. At the large cemetery of El-Hagarsa, on the west bank of the river opposite Akhmim, only two tombs were found undisturbed. While one tomb contained two coffins, the other had six. Each coffin preserved the remains of a man or a woman, wrapped in linen with very rudimentary mummification. There was no evidence of wealth in these tombs; just a couple of pottery jars, a spear and two bows and arrows. Despite the fact that the titles inscribed on the coffins show the owners as belonging to the aristocracy, theirs was a difficult and impoverished period of internal fighting and famines at the end of Dynasty 8, just before the complete collapse of the Old Kingdom.

For the plunderers to protect themselves against the tomb owner's wrath and revenge, they often mutilated his body or set it on fire. Destruction of the body, by fire or otherwise, meant a final extinction as it deprived the deceased's Ka from its abode. As a precautionary measure tomb owners furnished their tombs with one or more Ka statues which could act as a substitute for the body, and these were protected in a closed and inaccessible room, known now as 'serdab' (pls. 21, 22). However, tomb robbers broke into many of these serdabs, in most cases to damage not to steal the statues. Our recent excavations in the Teti cemetery at Saqqara provide ample evidence of the actions of tomb robbers, burnt bodies, complete bodies with missing heads, statues with broken necks, missing heads or defaced inscriptions. The same treatment of bodies is also met in the investigation of the tomb robberies in the Ramesside Period.

Usurpation of Tombs

Another threat to the tombs came from the usurpation of earlier tombs, or parts thereof, which, astonishingly, did not always take place a long time after the original construction. Unlike the tomb robbers, who stole the funerary possessions of a dead person to sell in secrecy, these usurpers were officials or even nobles, publicly reusing an already existing tomb after reinscribing it with their own name and titles, or quarrying away some stone from earlier tombs to use in the construction of their own resting places. It is difficult to understand the moral and legal justification of such public usurpations. Perhaps these actions should not be described as 'usurpation', possibly these tombs were abandoned in preference for larger ones when their owners were promoted or transferred. It is also possible that at the time of their reuse it was commonly known that these tombs had already been plundered and their owners' mummies entirely destroyed. Yet even so, reusing a tomb or quarrying away its stone was at least considered distasteful. In the First Intermediate Period, King Merikare's father instructed him:

> Do not despoil the monument of another, but quarry stone in Tura. Do not build your tomb out of ruins, using what had been made for what is to be made.

A few years earlier, Ankhtifi, a governor of the province of Moalla in Upper Egypt, boasted of the fact that he had applied this same principle:

> I have indeed acquired this sarcophagus and all parts of this tomb by my own means; for there is no usurped door, or usurped column in this tomb.

Hetepherakhti of Dynasty 5 and Nenki of Dynasty 6, among others, stressed the fact that they built their tombs in an empty place in the necropolis, in which no previous tombs existed. Both threatened anyone who would commit an evil action against their tombs, and Nenki curiously singled out

the officials and dignitaries who may cause any damage to any stone or any brick in his tomb.

The very mention of such declarations or threats suggests that transgressions against tombs were not uncommon. Archaeologists know only too well that stones have been removed from earlier tombs to be reused in more recent ones. Rather than erasing the existing decoration, these blocks were reversed and redecorated on the opposite side, an action which could only be exposed if the mastaba had totally or partially collapsed, allowing the different sides of its stone blocks to be seen. In some instances a name or title inscribed on the reverse side of the stone can indicate with certainty its origin from someone else's tomb. On the other hand, not all decorated blocks are automatically usurped, for cases are known of individuals building a second, larger tomb and reusing the same blocks from their own, earlier tomb. An example of this is the mastaba of Idi in the cemetery of King Pepy II at Saqqara and dating to the reign of this particular king. The excavator, Jequier, showed that the reused blocks in the annex to the burial chamber are from a previous tomb belonging to the same owner, who built the burial chamber itself with new blocks, probably with the intention of decorating it, which was never done. Perhaps he did not live to see the work on his new burial chamber achieved.

As a severe punishment for certain crimes some tomb owners and/or frequently members of their families had their names and figures systematically chiselled out from the decoration of their tombs. While this feature is sporadically attested in many cemeteries and from different periods, it is nowhere as evident as in the Teti cemetery at Saqqara. The damage does not appear to be the result of vandalism, as it is strictly limited to identity, name and figure, of the tomb owner, or to that of specific people shown in the tomb. With a possibly similar date for most of the individuals, it is not unlikely that they were implicated in the same crime, perhaps the assassination of King Teti himself which is only reported by the Egyptian historian Manetho of the Third Century BC, who stated that the king was assassinated by his bodyguards. The position of bodyguard is not clearly defined in the Egyptian hierarchy of officials but men, like Weni of Dynasty 6 who bears the title of 'palace attendant', described their responsibilities as providing protection for the king wherever he appears, which fits the role of a bodyguard. A number of men with this title who were buried in the Teti cemetery had their names and figures chiselled out from their tombs. Furthermore, a vizier named Hesi received the same

Fig. 8 Erasure of the tomb owner's figure and name, Hesi, Saqqara, Dynasty 6

treatment, and it is possible that he led, or was directly involved in, the conspiracy against the sovereign (fig. 8).

ONE PERSON, MULTIPLE ENTITIES

In order to understand the concept of death in a particular civilisation one has to understand what constitutes the human personality. According to the Egyptian beliefs, a person consisted of a number of different entities, all independent yet forming one being. Perhaps the most important of these was the Ka, a term which has been explained by scholars as 'personality', 'self', 'life-force', 'spirit', 'power', 'double', 'vital-force', etc.; perhaps it was all of these put together. In scenes of royal births we see the creator god Khnum, who fashioned human beings on the potter's wheel, shaping two identical figures of a child: the body and the Ka (fig. 9).

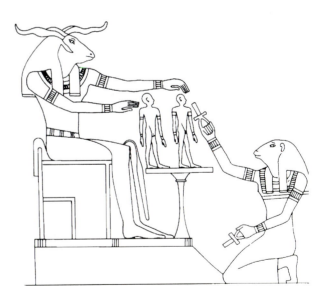

Fig. 9 Khnum fashioning the body and ka, Hatshepsut, Thebes, Dynasty 18

The Ka

The Ka existed in life as well as in the Hereafter. In life, all the person's activities were thought to be those of his Ka. Ptahhotep, for example, tells his son that 'the nobleman, when he is behind food, behaves as his Ka commands him'. He advises him: 'Do not malign anyone, great or small, the Ka abhors it', and also to enjoy the pleasures of life and not to do more than is required, for shortening the moments of pleasure 'offends the Ka'. Ptahhotep emphasises to his son the need to marry and produce a son: 'he is your son, your Ka begot him', and also advises him to act according to the wish of his superior for only then 'there will be peace from his Ka'. We can therefore conclude that the Ka was the person himself and was responsible for all his actions, behaviours, powers and achievements. During life the Ka was inseparable from the body and caused all its limbs, organs and faculties to function. Death was then seen as a temporary interruption to this union, which was overcome by preparing the body for an everlasting existence through mummification and the performance of the important rite of the 'Opening of the Mouth' which restored to the body its ability to eat, drink, breathe and speak, as well as regaining all its other senses. So important was this reunion between the body and its Ka that it became synonymous for death and resurrection. Thus Pepyseneb/Seni of El-Hawawish who decorated the tomb of his father after the latter's death, recorded his deed as: 'It was I who decorated this tomb for my father when he had gone to his Ka'.

In death it was the aspiration of each person that his Ka would remain with him, hence the inscriptions on the stela of Tjeti from the First Intermediate Period wish him a successful journey in the Hereafter 'His Ka being with him, his offerings before him'. A harpist's song to Nebankh of the Middle Kingdom wishes him a firm seat of eternity, and an everlasting monument filled with offerings: 'Your Ka is with you, it does not leave you'. As the dead person becomes associated with Osiris and other gods of the West, the Ka, even of ordinary individuals, seems to acquire a divine aspect and rather than representing it as simply two raised arms, ⊔ these are placed on a standard usually reserved for divinities ⊔. The difference between the Ka in life and in death is perhaps that in the latter state it was temporarily free to leave the body, lying in the burial chamber, to receive offerings presented to it in the tomb chapel, which was considered 'the Ka house'. As a kind of 'energy' the Ka needed constant nourishment, but as it did not travel far away from the tomb, offerings of food and drink had to be presented to the deceased in the chapel, otherwise the Ka could risk starvation. But as an 'energy' the Ka could travel from the burial chamber, where it rested in its body, through a deep shaft completely filled with sand and debris and through a monolithic stone false door to receive these offerings which were usually placed on an offering slab at the foot of the false door.

The Body

The second entity in the human being was his body, where his Ka dwelt all his life and continued to dwell in the Hereafter. Not only had the body all the limbs and organs of the person, but also it carried all his recognisable features and therefore represented his physical appearance, his form. For that reason the deceased's continued existence after death was dependent on the preservation of his body in a good, lifelike condition, and he was assured that 'your eyes are given you to see, your ears to hear, your mouth to speak, your legs to walk, your flesh is sound, there is nothing wrong with you'. Embalmers also constantly tried to perfect the art of restoring the original appearance by introducing resin or even mud under the skin in certain parts of the face and body to compensate for the effect of shrinkage through dehydration (see Mummification). But the Egyptian was aware that despite all his efforts the body could decay or be destroyed. As a precautionary measure the tomb was provided with one or more statues of the owner as a substitute for the body in such unfortunate circumstances. These statues, made of stone or wood, were of varying sizes and were mostly painted (pl. 6). Most of the statues represented the tomb owner in the prime of his life; others could also be included showing him at various ages, but always in perfect form. While the bodies of these statues were stereotyped and to a large extent idealised, a deliberate attempt was certainly made to individualise each face through genuine capturing of its semblance or at least by including its prominent characteristic features; for example, long face, big eyes, thick lips, moustache, etc. (pl. 21). The extent to which the statue represented a true image of its owner depended no doubt on the ability of the sculptor which varied considerably, between the superb and the crude, but regardless of the level of skill the artist seems to always have had his client in mind. So lifelike were some of these statues that the workmen involved in the excavation of the statue of Kaaper, now in the Egyptian Museum, Cairo, nicknamed it after Sheikh el-Balad 'the Elder of the village' because of their identical features (pl. 22). However, these statues were not art objects produced for artistic appreciation, but were rather funerary objects made for a utilitarian purpose. The statue was lifeless, in the same way as the body when it was separated from its Ka in death and before the 'Opening of the Mouth' ceremony was performed. Yet the same ceremony was conducted for each statue, in order to render it ready to receive the Ka, before it was placed in the tomb.

The Name

Another entity of the personality was the name; every person and everything has a name. In the Memphite Theology, for example, the God Ptah brought everything into being by pronouncing its name. A name was given to the individual at birth, identified them throughout their life and every effort was made to perpetuate it after death. It was important to know a person's name in order to wish them well or cause them harm. Thus the numerous offering formulae inscribed on false doors and on the walls of the tombs regularly end with the name, and titles for further identification, of the tomb owner. In the tomb of Iri/Tetiseneb in the Teti cemetery at Saqqara a formula written on the false door reads:

> An offering which the king gives and an offering which Anubis who is on his hill gives; that an invocation offering come forth for him, the nobleman of the king, Iri.

Another formula inscribed on the entrance lintel reads:

> An offering which the king gives and an offering which Anubis who is on his hill, foremost of the divine booth, who is in the embalming place, lord of the sacred land gives; that he be buried in the necropolis in the western desert, at a very good old age, as an honoured one before the king, the priest of the pyramid "One steadfast of places is Teti", Iri.

Pl. 6 Engaged rock-cut statues, Irukaptah, Saqqara, Dynasty 5

21

The name formed an essential element in one's identity, his very essence. For this reason it was necessary to inscribe the name of the tomb owner in front of every figure and on every statue representing him, regardless of the degree of the artist's success in portraying his features. Accordingly, the name was occasionally written more than ten times on the same false door appearing on every jamb, lintel, panel, etc. (fig. 10) Many individuals acquired additional names, perhaps bestowed on them throughout their career, some formed with the reigning king's name or that of a deity as an element; so Iri for example, became also 'Teti-seneb' and Sesi became 'Ankh-ma-hor'. While the original name was called 'the beautiful name', the later acquired ones were called 'the great names', and they too were regularly recorded since they reflected the latest status and identity of their owners.

Fig. 10
False door, Nedjetempet,
Saqqara, Dynasty 6

Erasing the name from the tomb scenes and inscriptions was a punishment inflicted on certain individuals, as thus one's other entities, physical and spiritual, would be condemned to a nameless existence in the Hereafter. A number of officials buried in the Teti cemetery seem to have conspired against the king and were duly punished (see above). However, the punishment differed between consistently erasing the tomb owner's name or erasing both his name and figure, possibly indicating two different sentences for two levels of criminal involvement.

Thus Semdent lost his name, while Seankhuiptah had both his name and figure systematically chiselled out. Yet, interestingly, enough remains in scattered spots in both tombs to allow reconstruction of their names and/or figures. One wonders if this reflects a mere inefficiency on the part of craftsmen responsible for the erasure, or a deliberate attempt to help the punished ones. If the latter, then the conspiracy must have had much broader dimensions.

Erasing names was not restricted to individuals; King Akhenaten expunged the names of gods, particularly Amun, in his attempt to spread his belief in the Aten as the only deity. The name and figure of Queen Hatshepsut were also removed from many places by her opponents after her death. Some kings, for example Ramesses II, appropriated buildings and statues belonging to their predecessors by simply erasing the old names and inscribing their own, without any attempt at altering the features of the statues or reliefs.

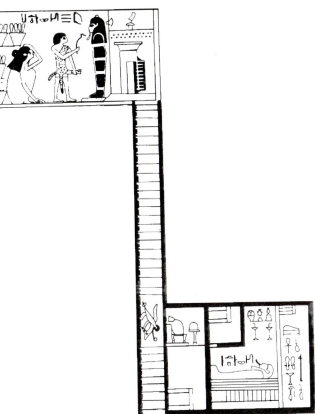

Fig. 11 The Ba descending the burial shaft, Papyrus of Nebqed

The Shadow

The concept of the shadow is less clear in Egyptian beliefs. It appears to be a state of power that can move with freedom and speed and is represented as a black figure of the deceased, a rather mysterious physical entity which manifests itself in different shapes and sizes.

The Ba

The Ba is a concept commonly associated with death and very rarely met in literature referring to the living. Ptahhotep for example says: 'The wise feeds his Ba with what endures, so that it is happy with him on earth.' In the 'Dispute between a Man and his Ba', from the First Intermediate Period, a man who suffers from life longs for death, but his Ba threatens to leave him, which could mean total annihilation. He entreats his Ba to remain with him and after a long dialogue between them the Ba agrees not to abandon him. The appearance of the

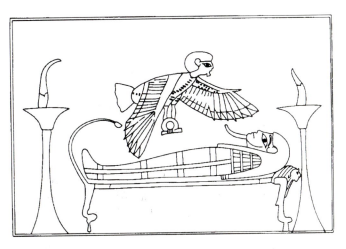

Fig. 12 The Ba hovers over the mummy, Papyrus Any, Dynasty 19

Ba at such a moment is understandable, since although still alive the man is contemplating death and about to depart. Similarly, when Sinuhe, the Egyptian official who fled the country in the Middle Kingdom, returned to Egypt and was ushered into the presence of the king, he described his condition as: 'I was like a man seized by darkness. My Ba was gone, my limbs trembled, my heart was not in my body, I did not know life from death'. This is the image of a man who has lost consciousness, in the same manner as the warning by one of the scribes that too much beer may result in the loss of the Ba.

The Ba is frequently translated as 'spirit', 'soul', 'power', etc., yet the Ba is one of the forms in which the deceased continues to live after death. It is represented as a bird, a jabiru stork, which from the New Kingdom was shown with the human head of the deceased. However, the Ba was believed to be able to take the shape or form it desired. With more freedom of movement than the Ka, which resides in the tomb, the Ba as a bird was able to travel through the world of the living as well as in the realm of the dead, and was able to wander on earth but also in the sky or the Netherworld. It left the tomb by day, could take any shape and perform physical activities including eating, drinking, or even copulating. But every night the Ba had to return and be reunited with its mummy in the burial chamber, in the underworld (fig. 11). Such a reunion was essential for its survival and was a worry for the deceased since the risk of the Ba losing its way or being somehow prevented from returning was always present. A special spell in the Book of the Dead aimed therefore at the safe return of the Ba. In the vignette accompanying the spell the Ba bird is depicted perched or hovering over its mummy with its wings stretched out in protection (fig. 12, pl. 23).

The Akh
Finally, the Akh, which in Egyptian means 'useful' or 'effective', is a concept that differs from all those preceding in that it did not represent a part or a form of the individual, but rather the individual himself in a state of 'blessedness'. An individual did not become an Akh simply by dying; but he had to successfully pass a great deal of physical and ritual practices necessary to render him an effective immortal. In rare circumstances an Akh can reach a higher order and become a 'God', as for example in the case of Isi of Edfu and probably Kagemni of Saqqara, both from the time of Teti. The inscriptions suggest that both individuals were deified after their death. Ascendancy in status in the

Hereafter and the ability to deal with other gods as well as with the living depended on knowledge of the heka 'magical rituals and spells'. Thus Ankhmahor of Saqqara warns the passer-by, by saying 'Never was any trustworthy magic hidden from me', and then threatens anyone who enters his tomb without purifying himself as he should for an excellent Akh saying 'I will seize his neck like a bird when the fear of me is cast in him, so that the Akhs and those who are upon earth may see it and may fear an excellent Akh. I will (also) enter into judgement with him in that noble council of the great god'. Like the Ba, the Akh was written with the hieroglyph of a bird, the crested ibis, Ibis Comata, but in pictures it was shown as a mummy. This might imply a combination of the freedom of movement and totality of form.

The Egyptian therefore believed that the individual was composed of many entities, all forming one being and all necessary for his existence. Some of these entities exist with him from his birth while others take shape only after he dies.

MUMMIFICATION

Early Mummification
The preservation of the body started accidentally when in the Predynastic Period bodies were buried in shallow graves, with some being preserved naturally through quick dehydration as a result of the heat and dryness of the sand. Towards the end of the Predynastic Period, and more so during the Dynastic era, tombs became more and more elaborate. Yet with the introduction of mud-brick lining of graves, followed by the excavation of deeper shafts leading to burial chambers into the rock level of the desert and the placement of the body inside a stone sarcophagus or a wooden coffin, any direct contact of the corpse with the hot, dry sand was prevented. This, in turn, resulted in its quick decomposition, unless an artificial method of preservation was employed. The method used in the first three dynasties was to wrap the body in linen bandages soaked in a resinous substance. These were moulded to take the shape of the face and body, sometimes with the limbs and genital organs wrapped individually. However, decomposition was not arrested as the internal organs were left in the body.

Incomplete Mummification

The Fourth Dynasty saw the beginning of two new developments in burial practices. First, some bodies were now buried in the extended position instead of the contracted, foetus-like position in use since the beginning of the Predynastic Period. Second, the need to remove the internal organs to help complete dehydration was realised; the earliest attested case of this practice being Queen Hetepheres, the mother of Khufu. However, there appears to have been a continuous development in the embalming techniques used during the Old and Middle Kingdoms, although the relatively few examples which have survived do not allow a detailed study of this. The evidence also suggests differences in the treatment of individual corpses. The body of Nefer buried in the Unis cemetery at Saqqara in the Fifth Dynasty (assuming that it belongs to the original tomb owner) was wrapped in linen in a semi-contracted posture and then completely covered with gypsum plaster. An examination of the remains of Nedjetempet, mother of the Sixth Dynasty vizier Mereruka, who owned a tomb near that of her son in the Teti cemetery at Saqqara, shows that the body was wrapped, but the wrappings are badly decayed with a charred appearance. Soft tissues are completely lacking and there is no evidence that the body was mummified. The bones were found loose but lay extended on the back in the correct anatomical position. As would be expected, no canopic jars were found, although such jars were not valued by tomb robbers and are accordingly found at Saqqara in tombs of this period where the owners have been mummified. The four jars were found, for example, in the neighbouring tomb of the vizier Inumin, although the sarcophagus was smashed and the body completely missing. The discovery at El-Hagarsa of an undisturbed burial chamber containing six bodies belonging to members of one family shed new light on the development of mummification. The six individuals, representing three generations, died violently at the end of Dynasty 8, during the turbulent years which brought the end of the Old Kingdom, and were accordingly buried together. The corpses were heavily wrapped in layers of cloth bandages and, with the exception of the two children, the four adults had their heads and breasts covered with cartonnage masks with all facial details as well as those of the wigs and breasts modelled and painted (pls. 7, 8). X-ray and endoscopic examination of these bodies revealed some interesting information. The bodies were certainly dehydrated, although they were not allowed to dry out completely before wrapping. As a result, the

Pl. 7 A male mummy, Hefefi, El-Hagarsa, Dynasty 8

Pl. 8 A female mummy, Hefefi, El-Hagarsa, Dynasty 8

remaining body fluids sank to the dependent parts of the mummy, the back or the left side according to its position in the coffin, staining the bandages and causing some deterioration and small holes. Such damage was also caused, at least in part, by insect activity in antiquity, some of which have been recognised in the samples obtained from the cavities and between the skin and bandages. While some of the soft tissues have been preserved, in most of the areas the bones have separated from their normal alignment primarily due to decomposition of the supporting soft tissue presumably as a result of inadequate dehydration. The rhinobase disruptions and the absence of brain fluid levels in at least two mummies indicate brain extraction, and proves that brain removal for mummification occurred at least 300 years earlier than previously attested. Curiously, however, no canopic jars for all six individuals were found. Yet the tomb shaft led to two burial chambers opposite each other, and while the chamber containing the coffins was undisturbed, the second chamber was opened and empty. Perhaps it contained the canopic jars and the funerary furnishings.

Mummification Perfected

From the Middle Kingdom onwards mummification techniques became much more efficient, but because of the availability of evidence, the picture is clearer for the New Kingdom and later. It is astonishing that despite the importance of the mummification process no record of its techniques has survived from ancient Egypt proper. Such lack of information may be related to the secrecy of this profession, which most probably remained within certain families. During the troubled times of the First Intermediate Period, Ipuwer laments the situation saying: 'Behold, those who were buried are cast on high ground; the embalmers secrets are thrown away'. Mummification was also linked to magic and Ipuwer says: 'Behold, magic spells are divulged; spells are made worthless through being repeated by people'. The only surviving written accounts of mummification are by the Greek historians Herodotus and Diodorus Siculus. The former describes three methods of mummification depending on cost and sophistication. Modern research shows that different methods were used in different periods and, in fact, great variations in techniques also existed at any one time.

The complete process of mummification included the removal of the viscera through an incision in the side of the abdomen. The same incision gave access to the lungs, the embalmer having to reach upwards through the diaphragm to reach the chest cavity. In some instances where the lungs have not been fully removed, they may be found either collapsed and lying close to the heart in the centre of the chest or still partly expanded and attached to the chest wall by adhesions. Either dehydrated or simply treated with natron (a type of salt) the extracted organs were preserved in a box known as the canopic box, which contained four compartments, or in the same number of canopic jars made of limestone or alabaster and containing the lungs, stomach, intestines and the liver. At first the canopic jars had flat lids, but in the First Intermediate Period the lids were made in the shape of a human head, probably to represent the deceased himself and in the New Kingdom these developed into heads representing the sons of Horus, the ape Hapy, the dog (jackal) Duamutef, the falcon Qebehsenuf, and the human Imsety, who had the role of protecting these organs (pl. 24). The jars with the organs were placed in the burial chamber, as they contained important parts of the body. In certain periods the organs were even wrapped and replaced inside the cavities of the body, or put on the mummy's legs.

Nothing in the surviving literature suggests that the Egyptians understood the function of the brain, and this was normally extracted through the nose by introducing a hook through the nasal passage, entering the cranial cavity through the base of the skull after breaking into the ethmoid bone. As brain tissue undergoes decomposition rapidly after death, becoming liquefied, it was flushed out of the nose, but residual brain tissue may be found in many cases as the ancient Egyptian clearly found it difficult to remove the brain in its entirety.

All parts of the body, whether in a liquid or solid form, as well as the materials which came into contact with it during mummification, were collected in what appears to be a shapeless sack, sometimes shown with a human head, called the tekenu. Some scenes show the transportation of the tekenu on a sledge, probably to be buried in the vicinity of the tomb (fig. 13). However, the tekenu has also been interpreted as an enigmatic figure which took part in the ceremony, although his/her exact role is uncertain.

The heart, tongue and kidneys were usually left in the body. The heart was believed to be the seat of intelligence (rather than the brain) and was therefore responsible for the individual's emotions, decisions and actions. In the Egyptian language the word heart 'ib' forms an element in many other words describing the human feelings and character; so happiness is 'sweetness of the heart' in Egyptian.

Fig. 13
The Tekenu on a sledge,
Ramose, Thebes,
Dynasty 18

Similarly it is an element in words like patience, courage, affection, desire, anxiety, determination, attention and wish. As such the heart represented the person's will, and indeed the person himself. In the final judgement in the presence of Osiris, it was the heart that was placed in the balance to be weighed against the feather of truth, justice and order, the Egyptian Maat. Alternatively, in some judgement scenes the heart was replaced by the complete figure of the deceased himself. The threat of the heart forsaking the person was present and one of the wishes for the deceased reads:

May you pass eternity in gladness and in favours
of the god who is in you. Your heart shall remain
with you, and it shall not forsake you.

In the 'Book of the Dead' the deceased addresses his heart as an independent entity saying:

O my heart of my being: Do not rise against me as
a witness,
Do not oppose me in the tribunal,
Do not rebel against me before the guardian of the
scales!

So important was the heart that in mummification it was either left in place or wrapped separately and replaced in the body. The tongue was also an important organ, for it was the heart's vehicle for expression. The kidneys on the other hand do not seem to have any religious significance, but because of their position in the body were presumably difficult to extract.

Following the removal of the internal organs, the whole body was dehydrated by using dry natron salt for approximately forty days. During this period the corpse was placed in a mummifying tub, a sloping bath with an opening at the lower end, all the body fats were dissolved and the liquids drained and collected for later burial, perhaps as part of the tekenu. It is interesting to note that the Egyptians had used dehydrating salts as a preservative method for food (such as fish) since early times. Cavities of the body were often stuffed with linen and resin to restore the original appearance, which was frequently achieved through the further introduction of resin or mud under the skin, mainly of the face. Finally, the abdominal incision was sewn up, the eye sockets were sometimes filled with linen and resin or with artificial eyes of stone, and the body was treated with spices and ointments or was insulated by applying resins to the skin before wrapping. A number of amulets could be inserted inside the body or between the layers of the bandages. The whole operation, including some religious rites, is said to have lasted for seventy days, although other estimates have been suggested. Thus in the Eighteenth Dynasty tomb of Djehuti at Thebes we read that 'A goodly burial comes in peace, when the seventy days are completed in the mortuary workshop', but the inscriptions in the tomb of Queen Meresankh III of Dynasty 4 show that the time she spent in the embalmer's workshop was 272 days, while that spent by the vizier Sendjemib/Inti of Dynasty 5 was at least one year (perhaps up to twenty months) while a tomb was being built by his son. Other cheaper and certainly faster methods of

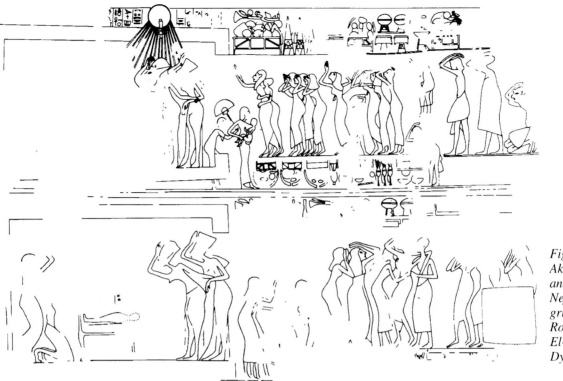

*Fig. 14
Akhenaten
and
Nefertiti
grieving,
Royal tomb,
El-Amarna,
Dynasty 18*

mummification, which did not require the surgical removal of the internal organs of the body also existed. Bodies treated in such ways were usually less well preserved.

FROM LIFE TO ETERNITY

While the moment of death is not represented in Egyptian tomb scenes, the journey from the family home to the final resting place is well illustrated although, as usual in Egyptian art, not all steps are depicted in every funerary scene. A few texts describing the funerary arrangements supplement our information on these practices, but it should be born in mind that these differed from one period to another in details.

Writing in the Fifth Century BC the Greek historian Herodotus described the initial shock reaction to death experienced by the Egyptians and their public expression of grief:

> In the case of people in whose houses there perishes a man of some consequence, all the females from these houses smear their heads with dust, and sometimes also the face, and then they leave the corpse in the house and themselves wander through the town and beat their breasts, with garments girt up and revealing their breasts, and with them all his female relatives. And the

males beat their breasts separately, these too with their garments girt up. And when they have done this, so do they carry forth the corpse to be mummified.

This initial episode of mourning is not depicted in scenes, perhaps because the body or coffin of the deceased did not play a role in it. The closest representation of such early grief is that of Akhenaten and Nefertiti in front of the dead body of their daughter Meketaten, but as it showed the king and his family, the expression is much more orderly (fig. 14).

The Funeral

We do not know what the deceased's family did during the relatively long period, seventy days or more, in which the corpse was in the embalming workshop. However, the sort of behaviour described by Herodotus was also demonstrated in the actual funeral procession which started from the deceased's house or the embalmer's workshop when the mummification was completed. This episode is vividly portrayed in a number of tomb scenes from all periods, as for example those in the Sixth Dynasty tombs of Mereruka and Ankhmahor at Saqqara and Idu at Giza and the Eighteenth Dynasty tombs of Ramose and Horemheb at Thebes.

The funeral procession of Any of Dynasty 19, depicted on his papyrus now in the British Museum,

28

also shows the same level of mourning (pl. 25). In the funeral of Ankhmahor of Saqqara the procession started from a structure, followed by the mourners (fig. 15). Fifteen women are in an extreme state of grief, hitting their faces and heads, raising their arms in

Fig. 15 Mourners, Ankhmahor, Saqqara, Dynasty 6

despair, sitting on the ground or collapsing and being helped by companions and one woman is tearing her dress in desperation. Eleven men are depicted separately, perhaps indicating the segregation of sexes in grief. These are in a state of deep sorrow, beating their heads, gesturing with their hands, comforting each other, crouching on the ground, one even fainting and being supported by companions. Two women still standing inside the structure shout: 'Oh my father, my lord, the kind one'. Despite all that, the scene is orderly in comparison with the more realistic and almost hysterical gesturing of mourners in scenes from the New Kingdom (fig. 16).

Preceding the mourners is the official party. The bier placed on wooden beams carried by men was followed by the chief celebrants. In the case of Ankhmahor there are four; a female 'djerit' - mourner, a seal-bearer of the god and chief embalmer, an embalmer of Anubis and a lector priest. While one 'djerit' - mourner is depicted in this scene, some other Old Kingdom funerals and certainly those of later periods show two females instead. These impersonate the goddesses Isis and Nephthys, the chief mourners of Osiris, which indicates that as early as the Old Kingdom the deceased was already identified with Osiris. As the procession had to cross the river, the inclusion of a seal-bearer of the god, who was responsible for boat transport, was essential. In the case of Ankhmahor the same

individual was also the chief embalmer. The second embalmer was called 'embalmer of Anubis', indicating the relationship of the profession to the god of burial. Embalming scenes from the New Kingdom show a man wearing the head-mask of Anubis handling the mummy. Finally came the lector priest, with a papyrus scroll in hand, who was responsible for reciting the appropriate religious and magical utterances capable of 'glorifying' a person, i.e., helping a mortal to become an Akh.

The itinerary of the funeral procession is best preserved in the Sixth Dynasty tomb of Pepyankh/Henikem of Meir, but may be complemented by scenes from the tombs of

Fig. 16 Female mourners, Ramose, Thebes, Dynasty 18

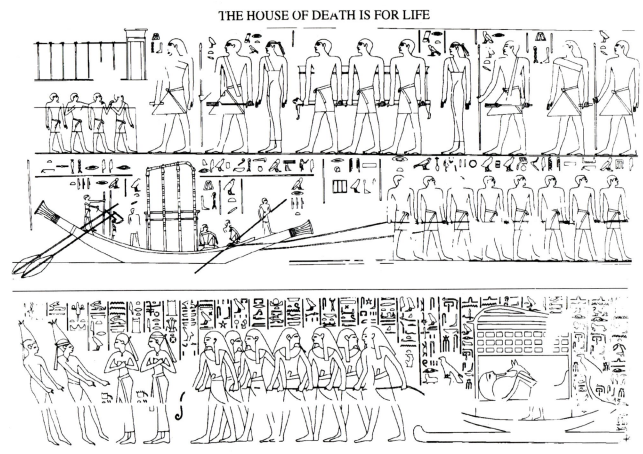

Fig. 17 (top) Funerary procession, Pepyankh/Henikem, Meir, Dynasty 6
Fig. 18 (bottom) Transporting the coffin, Rekhmire, Thebes, Dynasty 18

Mereruka at Saqqara, Qar and Idu at Giza, Tjeti, Tjeti-iker and Kheni at El-Hawawish, etc. After collecting the body from the embalmer's workshop the cortege had to make a river crossing. The coffin with the mummy, and frequently shrines containing statues of the deceased, were transported on barges of papyrus, or of wood in imitation of bound reed boats, which were pulled from shore or towed by large sailing boats (fig. 17). Whether these were simply crossing the river, usually to the west bank as most of the inscriptions indicate, or sailing in a pilgrimage to Abydos is uncertain. But it appears that it was during this trip that the lector priest recited his utterances before the deceased, and frequently his statues, aiming at 'glorifying' him, or making him an Akh.

Two false doors at Saqqara, those of Ptahhotep and Neferseshemre, provide us with the successive episodes through which the deceased went after leaving the embalming workshop. These read:

> Crossing the firmament in very good peace, going up to the top of the mountain of the necropolis, the grasping of his hand by his fathers, by his Kas and by every honoured person, making invocation offering for him on top of his burial apartment in his house of eternity, when he has reached a very good old age before Osiris.

> Going down into his house of eternity in very good peace, that his honour might be before Anubis, foremost of the west, lord of the sacred land, after an invocation offering has been made for him on top of his burial apartment, after traversing the lake and after he has been glorified by the lector priest, because of his very great honour before the great god.

The text indicates that after crossing the water and landing at the necropolis, the deceased went up the mountain of the necropolis. Scenes show us that the coffin and statues were carried on a sledge drawn by oxen or men and accompanied by dancers and funerary singers (fig. 18, pl. 26). The same picture appears in the text of Sinuhe from the Middle Kingdom where he is advised to think of his future burial as:

> A funeral procession is made for you on the day of interment, a mummy-case of gold with head of lapis-lazuli, with the heaven above you, as you are placed upon a sledge, oxen dragging you and singers in front of you, the dance of the mewew is performed at the door of your tomb, the requirements of the offering table are brought for you and there is sacrifice for you beside your offering stone.

30

The Eighteenth Dynasty inscription of Djehuti at Thebes describes the same rituals, which indicates their continuity through the centuries.

At the Tomb - The Opening of the Mouth

Arriving at the mouth of the shaft, frequently accessed from the roof of the tomb, the embalmers or more commonly the lector priest continued the rites of 'glorification' and 'Opening of the Mouth', which were followed by a huge meal. The Fourth Dynasty tombs of Debehni and Metjau of Giza and the Sixth Dynasty tomb of Kaihep/Tjeti at El-Hawawish depict this episode well. In the tomb of Debehni the funerary procession is shown ascending to the roof of the tomb, offering bearers are bringing food, sacrificial oxen are being slaughtered and dancers are performing (fig. 19). The 'Opening of the Mouth' was a rite of animation originally conducted on a statue of the deceased, but later presumably on the mummy itself. However, what is usually depicted in the New Kingdom is the anthropoid coffin, but it is uncertain whether it contained the actual mummy. The ceremony, which aimed at enabling the deceased to relive, to become an Osiris, by restoring his bodily functions, not only opening his mouth, but also his eyes, ears and nose, as well as reassembling his limbs, etc., became more complex with many priests participating, although the lector priest remained as the main officiant.

In its fullest form, the 'Opening of the Mouth' ceremony could extend over a period of days, but it is more likely that in most cases an abbreviated version was performed, including a selection of the more important rites. Although the ceremony was known at least as early as the Fourth Dynasty (the tomb of Metjen at Giza), the best representations of its rites come from the New Kingdom, for example in the Eighteenth Dynasty tomb of Nebamun and Ipuky at Thebes and the Nineteenth Dynasty papyri of Any and Hunefer now in the British Museum (fig. 20, pls. 25-7). These show the anthropoid coffin supported in a standing position by a priest sometimes wearing the head-mask of Anubis. One priest poured libation water over the coffin, and another, a sem-priest, touched the coffin, usually on the mouth, with an adze-like instrument, while a third priest recited texts for the rite. Mourners are usually depicted in the vicinity, and the wife is shown standing or kneeling at the feet of the coffin/mummy, in an obvious state of grief. Since the tomb was usually decorated during its owner's lifetime, the representation in the joint tomb of Nebamun and Ipuky of both their wives lamenting at the feet of their coffins is curious. Unless the

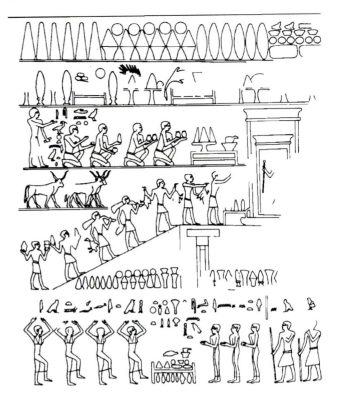

Fig. 19 Rites before the burial, Debehni, Giza, Dynasty 4

ceremony is held on empty coffins before they were placed into the burial chamber as part of the preparation of the tomb, one has to conclude that the two tomb owners predicted that they would die together and both be outlived by their wives. The involvement of the wife in the ceremony might also have religious significance in the same way as Isis took charge of Osiris' burial. Perhaps for the same reason a son was also present, representing Horus, son of Osiris. The meal at the mouth of the shaft

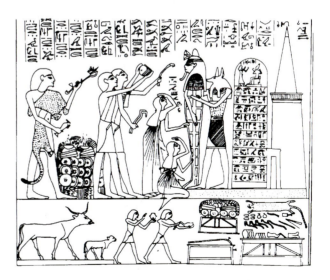

Fig. 20 Opening of the Mouth ceremony, Papyrus Hunefer, Dynasty 19

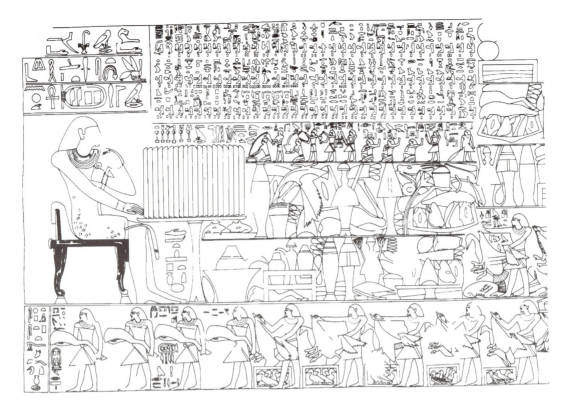

*Fig. 21
At the offering
table,
Pepyankh/
Henikem,
Meir, Dynasty
6*

was thus the deceased's first meal and was presented by the lector priest. This explains many sentences uttered by butchers and other workers involved in the preparation of food who are depicted in tomb chapels, for example: 'Hurry up! Bring the cut which the lector priest has requested', 'Hurry up,

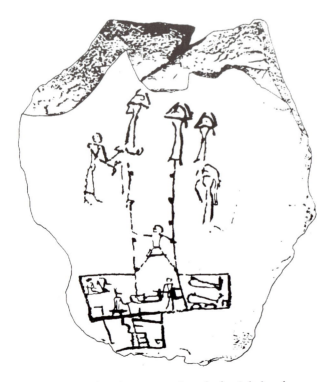

Fig. 22 Lowering the mummy into the burial chamber, ostraca

comrade! You must place this side of beef upon the altar, since the lector priest has arrived to perform the service'. The presence of the lector priest was essential, not only in the first meal but ideally for all future meals.

For this reason when Hardjedef of the Fifth Dynasty advised his son to build a tomb he also added that a priest should be appointed, for 'He profits you more than your own son; prefer him even to your heir', but frequently the person appointed his own son as his lector priest.

Invocation Offerings

Future meals were usually called 'invocation offering', a term which either means summoning the deceased to return to his offering table in order to receive the offerings brought for him, or summoning food and drink for the deceased (pl. 9). This 'call' is usually inscribed at the entrance of the tomb, on every false door and above the scenes of rows of offering bearers carrying items of food and drink and proceeding towards the false door or the offering table, with the hope that such supplies will continue in the future. To guarantee this the rich individual left a will assigning an estate, land and personnel, to provide for the 'invocation offerings'. Each of the meals was accompanied by a ceremony, which may be seen in the frequent representations of the tomb owner at the offering table, accompanied by an offering list naming all the required food and drink, and approached by offering bearers. In front of him are the persons performing the ceremony including two men libating, a lector priest glorifying and finally a man dragging a broom to remove the footprint of the officiants and close the services (fig. 21).

Following the completion of the glorification and the 'Opening of the Mouth' ceremonies the deceased goes to his Ka and becomes an Akh, a blessed one. His mummy was lowered into his burial chamber (fig. 22) and placed in the sarcophagus for better protection but the Ka was free to answer the calls for invocation offerings. Some tomb owners inscribed on the lid of their sarcophagi messages to the men who will be responsible for closing them, requesting them to do a perfect job.

Thus Ankhmahor of Saqqara said:

Oh 80 men, embalmer and administrator of the necropolis and every functionary who will descend to this place; do you desire that the king favours you, that invocation offerings come to you in the necropolis and your honour be well before the great god, then you should place for me this lid of this sarcophagus upon its mother (i.e. the chest) as efficiently as you are able, as that which you ought to do for an excellent Akh who did what his lord praised.

Pl. 9 Tomb owner requesting food, Kaaper, Saqqara, Dynasty 6

The men followed the instructions to the letter, even adding plaster to seal any gaps between the lid and the chest. Yet the lid was so heavy in itself that tomb robbers found it easier to break a hole through the side of the sarcophagus than to move the massive lid.

With the building of the tomb, the appointment of a priest, the allocation of land to provide the means for the funerary cult, the mummification, glorification and 'Opening of the Mouth' ceremonies, the Egyptian on earth did everything in his power for his future life. Yet that was not sufficient guarantee for eternity, he still had to pass the tests and to establish himself in the Netherworld.

IN THE REALM OF THE DEAD

With the completion of all the ceremonies, the mummy was interred, the burial chamber sealed and the second life began. Understanding the Egyptian afterlife is not a simple matter, for the Egyptian continuously added new concepts without discarding the old ones. The result was a number of beliefs, frequently contradictory, found side by side in the same text. Here however, only a broad outline of the main ideas can be given.

The Early Years - The Pyramid Texts

Little is known about the Egyptian view of the Hereafter during the earlier part of the Old Kingdom. It was not until Unis, the last king of Dynasty 5, that the burial chambers of kings and frequently queens were inscribed with the so-called Pyramid Texts (pls. 10, 11). Inscribed in vertical lines, these texts are formed of spells, the number of which varies according to the surface available in the burial chamber and the adjoining room. The total number of known spells is about 800, but no one pyramid records them all. These magical spells, which continued to be inscribed throughout the Sixth Dynasty, but whose usage was discontinued shortly after (they also sporadically appear in private tombs from different periods), must have been transmitted from much earlier traditions, perhaps even Predynastic.

References are made in these texts to burials in the sand, at a time when kings and queens were certainly buried in stone pyramids, with burial chambers excavated in the native rock or built of stone. Thus Utterance 373 says: 'Take your head, collect your bones, gather your limbs, shake the earth from your flesh', and Utterance 747: 'Stand up! Remove your earth! Throw off your dust!'

The spells may be divided into three main topics. The first was aimed at protecting the burial chamber itself from any creature, human or animal; the second was composed of funerary, offering and resurrection rituals performed on behalf of the deceased, while the third topic consisted of spells for the use of the king or queen aiming at helping them in their passage from life to the Hereafter.

The Pyramid Texts exhibit a mixture of heavenly beliefs, for the dead king could have an astral afterlife among the circumpolar stars, or a solar one in the company of the sun-god Re, or even in the company of Osiris who sometimes was given a place in the sky. The main purpose of the texts was therefore the resurrection of the king, his ascent to the sky and his admission to the company of other gods. Utterance 245 says:

> Make your seat in heaven, among the stars of heaven; for you are the Lone Star, the comrade of Hu! You shall look down on Osiris, as he commands the spirits, while you stand far from him. You are not among them, you shall not be among them!

Whether these royal prerogatives were passed on to the nobility and the officials of the Old Kingdom is not known. Certainly they also believed strongly in an afterlife and prepared for it, but a detailed explanation of their notion of the Hereafter has nowhere survived. The above-mentioned Utterance 245 of the Pyramid Texts confirms Osiris' command of spirits, other than royal, in an earthly afterlife. Osiris, the god of the dead, appeared in funerary formulae in the latter part of the Old Kingdom as, for example, in the offering formula saying:

Pl. 10
Pyramid Texts, Teti burial chamber, Dynasty 6

An offering which the king gives and an offering which Osiris, lord of Busiris gives; that he (i.e., the deceased) may be buried well in his tomb in the necropolis of the western desert... .

However, the role of Osiris here is unclear. Although possible, we should not automatically assume that a belief in the judgement of the deceased by a court of deities headed by Osiris, as was the case in later periods, also existed in the Old Kingdom.

The Coffin Texts

The collapse of the Old Kingdom, the relatively unstable time that followed, known as the First Intermediate Period, and the rise of rival monarchs from among commoners accelerated the transferral of many of the royal prerogatives to the nobility and officials. As a result, from the First Intermediate Period funerary texts began to be inscribed in ink inside the wooden coffin, a tradition which became characteristic of the Middle Kingdom (fig. 23). The texts consist of spells partly taken from the Pyramid Texts, with many new additions aiming at assisting the deceased in his afterlife. The new section is described as 'Guides to the Hereafter' and is often accompanied by a map. This describes the obstacles and the inhabitants of the Netherworld and the words to be said in order to gain passage. One of these Guides is called 'The Book of Two Ways'.

From these texts, written in hieratic, it is noticeable that Osiris began to be accorded pre-eminence over other deities as god of the Netherworld, although the others still retained a presence and influence. The dead was now, as he might have been earlier but evidence is lacking, expecting to live in a kingdom ruled by Osiris, and in fact he was identified with this god. So from the Middle Kingdom onwards, writing 'the Osiris' before a person's name was equivalent to describing him as 'the deceased' or 'the late'.

The Coffin Texts speak of the deceased continuing his afterlife in the Field of Reeds, an ideal rich and fertile land in the Netherworld, similar to the land of Egypt, only better. We have no evidence from the Old Kingdom of the presence of such an idea, which may have been a later development of the funerary beliefs. Perhaps this arose from the Egyptian's observation through the centuries that his total reliance upon the earth and the living for sustenance after death, and the funerary arrangement that he made, were neither perpetual nor secure. But, unlike life on earth, the deceased had to work in the Field of Reeds, particularly in relation to agricultural tasks. Scenes from later periods show the tomb owner, sometimes

Pl. 11 *Pyramid Texts, details, Teti, Dynasty 6*

accompanied by his wife, ploughing in these fields (pl. 28). To replace him in such duties, as was the case in his lifetime, workers represented by small figurines called shabtis (or ushabtis) were buried with the deceased. These were made of wax, wood, stone or ceramic, and were buried in the tomb, sometimes as many as one figurine for each day of the year. Figures of overseers, wearing different types of kilts, were also added. Wooden tomb models and funerary figurines became common in the Middle Kingdom. These represent boats, granaries, houses and figures of workers in different

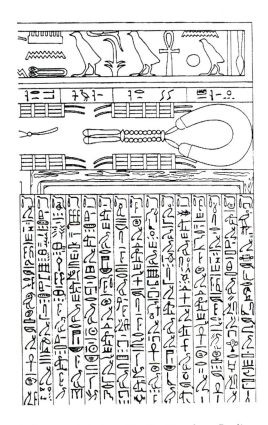

Fig. 23 *Coffin text, Sebekaa, Middle Kingdom, Berlin Museum*

professions including soldiers. But figures could also represent the deceased in a mummy form which was placed in a model coffin and deposited in the tomb, in a temple or at Abydos. The idea was for the statuette to replace the body if it were destroyed, or partake in offerings and rites made in temples. In general the spread of the cult of Osiris and the simplification in burial customs in the Middle Kingdom made it more feasible for less wealthy individuals to aspire to an eternal life.

The Book of the Dead

The New Kingdom saw the appearance of more funerary literature. From the Coffin Texts were developed 'Guides to the Hereafter', books which included the Amduat (or that which is in the Netherworld), the Book of Gates, the Book of Caverns, the Book of Earth, etc. These books were first inscribed and illustrated in royal tombs at Thebes and later appeared on private papyri and sarcophagi. They all have as a common theme the journey of the sun during the night until it is reborn at dawn. The destination of the sun at night offers contradictory concepts; in one the sun is believed to be swallowed every evening by the sky goddess Nut

Fig 24 Nut and Geb

and travels through her body to be reborn as a rejuvenated child in the morning. In a different concept the sun goes down by night into the waters of the primeval ocean, the Nun, or into the Netherworld, the realm of the dead, and lightens its darkness before it rises again on the world in the morning; its arrival in a renewed form being celebrated and announced by four baboons. The contradiction in these beliefs is such that in one concept the sun remained above earth at night, while in another it went underground. The sky goddess Nut was shown as a female bending over the earth god Geb (fig. 24), thus travelling inside her body

was travelling above earth, while sailing on the lower sky was underground. The lower sky was thought of as a counterpart, a reversed version of the one above earth and was interestingly written with a reversed determinative ⌐⌐ as against the usual ⌐⌐ .

The Netherworld was a land of pitfalls and dangers, and a knowledge of its topography and inhabitants was essential for the dead in order to safely accompany the sun on its journey. For this he needed to be provided with all the necessary 'Guides' for the region. These contain not only the description of the Netherworld in words and pictures, but also spells and instructions on what to say or do in each situation. Even an innocent person may be caught in the perils of the Hereafter; his Ba may lose its way or be trapped in a net, one of the terrible doorkeepers at the different gates in the Netherworld might refuse to let him pass, etc. (pls. 29, 30). The books describe this land as divided into twelve sections, which correspond to the twelve hours of the night. The beginning of these twelve sections represent neutral ground between life and death. In the middle, however, the sun descends into a deep, dark valley, referred to as the place of destruction, inhabited by the enemies of gods and those who failed to pass the final judgement test (see below). They are depicted decapitated, bound and burnt by snakes and other divine creatures spitting fire, or instead being boiled in a cauldron, thus facing a possible extinction (figs. 25, 26). However, Egyptian religion seems to be based on both fear and hope. After Osiris was murdered and cut up by his brother Seth, he came back to life, and gave hope to everyone, since every dead person could theoretically become an Osiris. In the depth of the underworld was a large primeval body of water, the Nun, where even those who were not properly buried or mummified could drown and be reborn.

The sun god, shown as a human with a ram's head (the ram being another phonetic writing of the Ba), sails in his boat on a river that runs through the Netherworld as a counterpart for the Nile (fig. 27). He spends one hour in each of the twelve sections, during which the dead in this section come to life, remove their protective mummy bandages, greet the sun god and other deities and resume all activities including cultivating fields. However, time in the Hereafter is different from that on earth, an hour in the first is the equivalent of a lifetime in the second. The sun god in his boat then leaves one section for the next, until his nightly journey is completed at dawn. While in the Netherworld Re is assimilated with Osiris, becoming Re-Osiris or the Ba of Osiris,

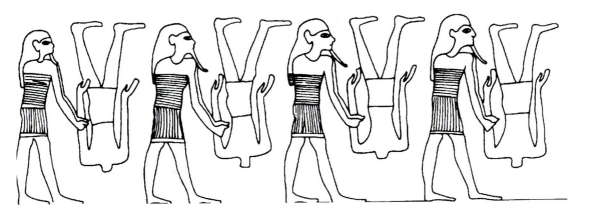

Fig. 25 Punishment in the underworld

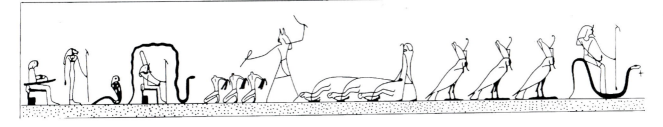

Fig. 26 Punishment in the underworld

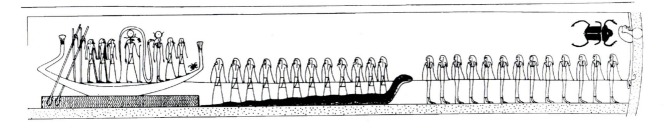

Fig. 27 The sun god in the Netherworld

and like these two gods the dead was able to experience two realms: as a Ba he could fly in the sky, and as a body, Ka and shadow he was bound to earth. But despite the partial reliance of the dead on the living, and the ability of the dead to enjoy life's manifestations, life in the Hereafter was not on earth, but in one of the two realms where he comes face to face with the gods.

When the dead has passed all the gates and perils of the Netherworld he arrives at the Judgement Hall. The Book of the Dead, known to the Egyptians as 'the Coming Forth by Day' is our main source of this judgement. Descending from the Pyramid Texts and the Coffin Texts, the Book of the Dead appeared in its classical form in Dynasty 18, although earlier versions do exist, and it remained in use until the Graeco-Roman Period. Written (usually in hieroglyphic script) on papyrus, and therefore available at perhaps a reasonable cost, the Book of the Dead is composed of any number of spells

chosen from some two hundred known and now numbered by modern scholars. High quality copies were especially written for wealthy individuals, while more cheaply, mass produced versions for those with lesser means frequently contain errors and omissions. The prospective owner had only to add his name. In addition to the spells, the papyri containing the Book of the Dead also include some illustrations representing various aspects of life in the Netherworld, and some of these vignettes and spells found their way also into the repertoire of tomb scenes and inscriptions, particularly in those of the Ramesside Period at Deir el-Medina in Thebes.

Although a Hereafter in the company of Re is mentioned in the Book of the Dead, Osiris is certainly supreme. The book contains spells, or chapters, designed to guide the deceased in various situations and to help him achieve resurrection. There are chapters for the 'Opening of the Mouth', for keeping one's head, for obtaining air and water by the Sycamore tree, etc. Chapter 30B for example reads:

The heart as witness:
Spell for not letting the heart of .... oppose him in the necropolis.
He shall say:

O my heart of my mother (i.e. the one I was born with),
O my heart of my mother, O my heart of myself.
Do not stand against me as witness.
Do not oppose me in the tribunal.
Do not rebel against me before the guardian of the scales.

Judgment of the Dead

Pl. 12 Osiris and the forty-two judges, New Kingdom Papyrus, Egyptian Museum, Cairo

One of the longest chapters and perhaps the most important is Chapter 125, which deals with the final judgement of the dead. The judgement took place in the Hall of the Two Truths, named as such after the forty-two gods/judges (pl. 12), who represent the various aspects of order/truth/justice, the Egyptian concept of Maat, and who sit in the hall in two rows facing each other. Osiris, god of the dead, presides over the judgement. It is interesting that Egypt was divided into two regions and these were formed of forty-two provinces. The deceased entered the hall, led by Anubis who was originally responsible for his mummification. He starts his speech by an address to Osiris:

Hail to you, great god, lord of the Two Truths!
I have come to you, my lord, I was brought to see your beauty.
I know you, I know the names of the forty-two gods,
who are with you in the Hall of the Two Truths ... .

The deceased then declares his innocence from his sins such as:

I have not committed crimes against people,
I have not mistreated cattle,
I have not done any harm,
I have not robbed the poor,
I have not done what the god abhors,
I have not caused pain,
I have not caused tears,
I have not killed,
I have not ordered to kill, ...

No evil shall befall me in this land,
in the Hall of the Two Truths;
for I know the names of the gods in it,
the followers of the great god.

The deceased then addresses the forty-two gods, each by his name and denies having committed the sin that this judge examines. For example:

O Wide-of-stride, who comes from On: I have not done evil.
O Shadow-eater, who comes from the cave: I have not stolen.
O Savage-faced, who comes from Rostau: I have not killed.

Many other sins are denied including greed, lies, ill-temper, adultery, homosexuality, arrogance and ignoring the truth.

This judgement is usually called by scholars the Negative Confession, because the deceased was only required to deny sins and not to declare his good deeds during his lifetime. This does not mean that benevolence on earth was of little importance, but this was not judged by the gods, but by the people themselves on earth. Thus the deceased left inscriptions in prominent places in his tomb stating his kindness, generosity and positive actions while alive, hoping that these would be reciprocated by those who follow him on earth.

The deceased's heart, as the seat of intelligence, will and memory, was weighed against the feather of Maat, goddess of truth, justice and order (fig. 28, pl. 31). The scale was attended by the jackal-headed Anubis, and the verdict was recorded by the ibis-headed Thoth, who was known for his exactitude

says in the tribunal. Accordingly, the scales of the balance were always in equilibrium or even showed a lighter heart than the feather of Maat. A favourable verdict was written by Thoth and delivered to Osiris and the judges, who finally declare their judgement. In the case of Any this says:

> Words spoken by the Great Ennead to Thoth who
> dwells in Hermopolis:
> What you have said is true. The Osiris scribe Any,
> justified, is innocent.
> He has committed no crime nor has he acted
> against us.
> Ammit shall not be permitted to prevail over him.
> Let there be given to him of the offerings which
> are presented to Osiris
> and a permanent grant of land in the field of
> offerings as for
> the followers of Horus.

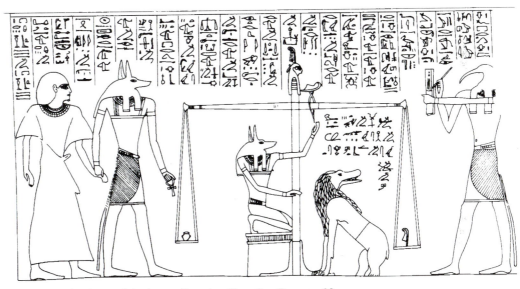

Fig. 28 Weighing of the heart, Papyrus Hunefer, Dynasty 19

and precision. Sometimes two hearts, those of the man and his wife, were weighed together against two feathers, perhaps reflecting the desire to share the same lot in the Hereafter, or their joint responsibility for their actions on earth. A composite monster named Ammit, which had the head of a crocodile, the forepart of a lion and the hindpart of a hippopotamus, was on hand near the balance ready to gobble up the heart should it fail to pass the test. But she is never depicted as actually devouring a heart. The Book of the Dead had planned a safe passage through every situation, the weighing of the heart included. We have seen that Chapter 30B made sure that the deceased's heart would not stand against him and oppose what he

The deceased was then declared 'justified' or 'true of voice', i.e., what he said concerning his behaviour on earth was correct, and was admitted to the kingdom of Osiris, or he himself became an Osiris. This, however, does not at all indicate that the dead reached the same status as the gods, but merely that through death and resurrection he was able to enjoy the renewing life originally reserved for the gods.

SUSTENANCE AND REMEMBRANCE FOREVER

Pl. 13 Representation of funerary estates, Hesi, Saqqara, Dynasty 6

Pl. 14 False door of Iteti, Giza, Dynasty 5, Egyptian Museum, Cairo

Death according to the ancient Egyptian did not end his physical needs. He required sustenance and enjoyed many activities including sexual pleasures in life and would continue to do so after death. Multiple sources of food and drink were organised or requested on earth and others were believed to have existed in the Netherworld. Not all these sources served the same purpose, nor were they superfluous substitutes in case some of them failed to materialise. The human being was believed to consist of multiple entities in life, to which were added new ones which came into existence after death. These entities experienced different destinies, in the grave, in the underworld, among the stars, or accompanying the sun-boat, etc. These are not contradictory conceptions, for they address the multiple facets of the human personality. Provisions were also needed for different entities in different places. Food and drink on earth were required to be given by the living for the nourishment of one's Ka, yet the Ka continued to exist in the Hereafter, only less closely tied to the body. Its needs, however, remained the same and their fulfillment remained on earth, in the tomb chapel, the house of the Ka. But as an Akh the deceased started a new life in the underworld and there he needed new sources of sustenance and this was in the Field of Reeds.

Funerary Estates

For supplies to continue on earth, the rich Egyptian endowed a funerary estate to provide for his funerary services. The endowment consisted usually of a piece of agricultural land and a number of priests and farmhands. In many cases the eldest son was appointed as the lector priest and/or the executor of the tomb owner's will. Such appointments were not only out of strong family ties which characterised the Egyptian civilisation, but were based on religious grounds since Horus, son of Osiris, buried his father and performed the funerary rites. The wills included the proviso that the neglect of any of the father's requirements would disinherit the son. Thus Qereri of El-Hawawish, Dynasty 6, wanted a garden opposite his tomb and he wrote:

> I came indeed to the necropolis, I dug out a basin of 100 cubits on each side, with 10 sycamores on it (i.e., on each side). As for any of my sons who shall neglect these, he will have no claim to any of my possessions.

As this text indicates, more than one son could be involved, and indeed a number of priests and Ka-servants may be appointed to serve for a certain period every year in a system of rotation in return for a share of the income. Nikaankh, a priest of Hathor in the Fifth Dynasty, appointed twelve members of his family to carry out the duties, one for each month of the year.

Records of some funerary estates exist in tomb chapels of the wealthy officials, where each estate is represented in the decoration of the chapel by a female offering bearer in front of whom the estate's name is inscribed (pl. 13). As many of the estates carry names formed with a king's name as an element and since the same estate frequently appears in more than one tomb, it is likely that some of the estates were royal and that the kings offered certain favoured officials the privilege of receiving offerings from them. Priests and Ka-servants had the responsibility of performing the funerary rites and of placing the offerings on the offering slab in front of the false door in the chapel. Being an 'energy' or a 'life force', the Ka was able to ascend from the burial chamber where it dwelt in its body, to rise into the shaft's filling and to come through the false door in order to receive the offering. The central panel of the false door usually contains an image of the tomb owner at an offering table and, since as a substitute for the body the Ka can dwell in a statue or even a figure, such an image can house the Ka while consuming the offerings. Some false doors also incorporate a statue for the same purpose (pl. 14); thus Neferseshemptah of Saqqara had a standing statue in a niche on either jamb and a third statue, but only a bust, in the panel (pl. 15). In a most revealing representation, Idu of Giza positioned his bust statue in the lower part of the central niche of

Pl. 15 Statue in false door, Neferseshemptah, Saqqara, Dynasty 6

his false door, depicting him coming through the door to receive offerings with his open hands placed on the offering-slab, palms up.

Offerings by the Living

For further guarantee of continuous sustenance, tomb owners inscribed on the entrance of their tombs an account of their virtues and deeds while on earth, then requested the passers-by to place some offerings from whatever they possessed, or simply to verbally ask for offerings for the tomb owner and to accompany that with a specific offering gesture by the hand. Thus Kaaper of Saqqara wrote on his entrance jamb:

> Beloved of the king and beloved of Anubis, who is on his hill, is any person or Ka-servant who shall pass by this road in travelling downstream or upstream. Pour water for me and give bread and beer to me from that which is in your possession. If there are no bread and beer and water in your possession (then) shall you say with your mouth and make gesture with your hand: a thousand of bread and beer, a thousand of r-geese, a thousand

of *trp*-geese, a thousand of *zt*-geese, a thousand of *sr*-geese, a thousand of pigeons, a thousand of oryxes, a thousand of oxen and pure incense for the overseer of the workcentre, the royal chamberlain, the overseer of the great court, the honoured one before the king, before Anubis who is on his hill, and before the great god lord of the west (pl. 9).

The appeal by the Egyptians to those still living to recite these so-called 'invocation offerings' at the door of their tombs was based on the belief in the power of the spoken word, which, like the written one, could magically produce benefit or harm to the one for whom it was pronounced. Pronouncing the 'invocation offering' formula for the deceased also acted to summon his Ka to come and receive the offering. In order to encourage people to utter such a formula for him, Paheri, a mayor of El-Kab in the Eighteenth Dynasty, inscribed all his virtues and achievements in his tomb, for example:

> I did not neglect making payment in full,
> I did not take a slice of the expense.
>
> My good character raised me high,
> I was summoned as one who is blameless.
>
> I told no lie to anyone.
> I was a model of kindliness.

He then asks the people to recite for him the offering formula, in fact simply to read it as written in the tomb:

> Say "An offering which the king gives", in the form in which it is written, "An invocation offering" as said by the fathers.

Interestingly, he tells the people that such a recital does not cost them anything, but is of great benefit to him:

> I say to you, I let you know:
> It is a recital without expense,
> It does not make poor, it makes no trouble;
> It means no quarrel with another,
> It is not coercing one who is needy.
> It is a pleasing speech that uplifts,
> The heart does not tire to hear it.
> The breath of the mouth, it is not eaten,
> There is no strain, no fatigue in it.
> It is good for you when you do it,
> You will find in it [profit] and praise.
> While I was in the land of the living,
> No sin against god reproached me.
> I have become an equipped, blessed spirit,
> I have furnished my place in the graveyard.
> I have what I need in all things,
> I shall not fail to respond.
> The dead is father to him who acts for him,
> He forgets not him who libates for him,
> It is good for you to listen!

Other examples of the same idea exist, as in the inscriptions of Harwa from the Late Period who says:

> The breath of your mouth profits the silent,
> without cost to your possessions.

Permanent Offerings

Tombs also contained scenes showing the production of food and drink and it has been argued that through magical formulae these come into reality (see below). Long lists of offerings, which include various types of bread, cake, beer, wine, different birds and cuts of meat, were inscribed near the offering table scenes and were frequently accompanied by a scene of priests performing the offering ritual. The names of these items, recited by a priest or a visitor, were believed to bring them into existence and, in fact, similar lists were sometimes written on the walls of burial chambers, as were scenes of food and drink items such as in the Saqqara tombs of Inumin and Idut (pl. 64). These scenes and inscriptions in the burial chamber probably aimed at nourishing the Ka without having to ascend to the chapel.

But sustaining the deceased was not restricted to his tomb, since the Ka could theoretically be called upon, by pronouncing its owner's name, to receive offerings elsewhere. Therefore, placing a funerary stela or a statue with an offering formula written on it in a royal mortuary temple, or even the tomb chapel of a distinguished and deified individual, allowed its owner to partake of the offerings regularly presented in this temple or tomb. One of the most common places for such cenotaphs was the 'Terrace of the Great God' at Abydos, the cult centre of Osiris; but tombs of individuals such as Kagemni of Saqqara, Isi of Edfu and Hekaib of Elephantine were also popular.

Funerary Feasts

A number of feasts were celebrated every year by the living, during which times food and drink were apparently served in abundance. Not wanting to miss out on such special occasions, tomb owners inscribed in a prominent place in their chapels a request for 'invocation offerings' on such days which they specifically named. Thus Neferseshemre of Saqqara wrote on his false door:

> An offering which the king gives and Osiris, lord of Abydos, gives; that he receives his invocation offerings at the opening of the year feast, the Thoth feast, the first of the year feast, the Wag-feast, the Sokar feast, the great feast and at every feast and every day, to the length of time.

Texts from the Old Kingdom also mention other feasts, such as the monthly feast, the half-monthly feast, the coming forth of Min feast, etc. There were twelve festivals in total, which were later expanded to more than twenty.

As an example of these feasts, the Wag-feast was celebrated on the 18th of Thoth, the first month of the inundation season and was dedicated to Osiris. Cattle were sacrificed on the day and the dead man was wished a successful voyage to Abydos. Another important feast was 'the beautiful feast of the desert valley', held in Thebes in the New Kingdom, particularly in Dynasty 18, in Payni, the second month of summer. On this occasion, the divine barque of the god Amun was transported from his temple at Karnak to the west bank to visit the mortuary temples of kings. Ordinary people celebrated the day in joyous activities in the cemeteries near the tombs of their loved ones. In this way the dead were able to enjoy the feast together with members of their families in the tombs which became 'houses for the joy of the heart'.

Fig. 29 The tree-goddess nourishing the deceased, Sennedjem, Dynasty 19

Tree-goddess

The goddess Hathor was believed to be present in the festival and indeed she played an important role in the life of the deceased. As a tree-goddess she nourished the deceased and provided him with refreshing drink. She was represented as a tree, mostly a sycamore, with a woman's body growing from it.

The deceased, frequently accompanied by his wife, is shown sitting under or near the branches of this tree and enjoying the fruit and drink it offered such as in the Theban tomb of Sennedjem (fig. 29). Scenes and inscriptions clearly show a link between the tree-goddess, the symbol of renewal, and the dead in the form of a Ba; for as a bird he was attracted to, and nourished by, the tree. Both men and women were associated with Hathor, but in later periods while dead men were Osirified, women were identified with Hathor. But Hathor was above all a sky-goddess, and in the Coffin Texts the deceased says: 'Hathor reach me with your hand, so that you may take me up to the sky'. In the same way Hathor was a goddess of the nocturnal sky and as such had an important role as a goddess of the dead. In these roles she had a great deal in common with the sky goddess Nut.

Finally, the deceased after passing judgement, declared justified and becoming an Akh, was given a piece of land to cultivate in the Netherworld, the Field of Reeds (also called Field of Rushes). He is frequently depicted, sometimes accompanied by his wife, performing all sorts of agricultural activities, including ploughing, sowing, treading out the seeds and harvesting. This is shown in the New Kingdom tomb of Sennedjem. The Egyptian envisaged the Netherworld to be similar to this world with its waterways, islands and land (pl. 28). There everything was abundant, including the flood waters and the harvest, but the same hard work required on earth was again expected. Chapter 110 of the Book of the Dead and the vignette that accompanied it regularly describe and illustrate the land. Part of this chapter reads:

43

Here begin the spells of the Field of Offerings and spells of going forth into the day; of coming and going in the realm of the dead; of being provided for in the Field of Rushes which is in the Field of Offerings, the abode of the Great Goddess, the Mistress of Winds; having strength thereby, having power thereby, ploughing therein, reaping and eating therein, drinking therein, copulating therein, and doing everything that used to be done on earth by ... (Name).

Permanent Servants - Ushabtis

To replace the deceased in the hard labour in these fields, ushabti figurines were provided and were believed to magically act as a substitute for the deceased himself, although later they came to be regarded as mere servants. A special spell for this purpose appeared in the Middle Kingdom Coffin Texts, and from the New Kingdom the figurines were inscribed with Chapter 6 of the Book of the Dead that reads:

> Oh Ushabti, allotted to me, if I be summoned or if I be detailed to do any work which has to be done in the realm of the dead; if indeed obstacles are implanted for you therewith as a man at his duties, you shall detail yourself for me on every occasion of making arable the fields, of flooding the banks or of conveying sand from east to west; "Here am I", you shall say.

Placing in tombs model statuettes of workers in various professions was common during the Middle Kingdom, although earlier and later examples are known. The ushabtis presumably represent a similar concept, but were mainly aimed at performing agricultural tasks in the Netherworld (pl. 16).

Tomb owners were accustomed to having labourers performing such duties for them during life and expected such a privilege in death. For this reason the figurines are frequently represented

Pl. 16 Ushabti figures, Museum of Ancient Cultures, Macquarie University

carrying a hoe and a pick and with a basket suspended on their back. Ushabtis were made of various materials, wax, clay, wood, stone, rarely bronze, but the most common was faience. The number of figures buried with the deceased depended on his/her wealth, but numbers also increased in time to reach 401, consisting of 365 workers, one for each day of the year, and 36 overseers, the latter wearing triangular kilts traditionally worn by higher officials and holding whips. With these numbers, ushabtis became mostly mass produced, frequently with indistinguishable features.

Achievements

Food and drink were not all that the deceased hoped to receive from the living, for they wished to be remembered among them, to be talked about and to have their name live forever on earth. This was so fundamental to the ancient Egyptian that they tried to record for posterity everything they did in their lifetime. The tomb itself, in addition to being an eternal house for the deceased and a place where their funerary rites could be maintained, was a memorial for their earthly activities and achievements. Whoever could afford the expense left scenes in their tomb chapel, which they expected to be visited, related not only to the production of food and other necessities but also to some great moments in their career, which could include scenes of war, receiving a foreign delegation, being rewarded with the gold of honour, or the like. Thus war scenes appear for example in the Fifth Dynasty tomb of Inti at Deshasha and the Eleventh Dynasty tomb of Khety at Beni Hasan. Djehutihotep of the Twelfth Dynasty, on the other hand, depicted in his tomb at El-Bersha, the transportation of his colossus statue, etc. Such scenes were obviously of no direct benefit to the deceased in his future life but were an impressive reminder for future generations of his achievements.

Biographical inscriptions listing the highlights of the owner's career are known from all periods, frequently inscribed in a most conspicuous place in the tomb (pl. 17). The vizier Sendjemib/Inti inscribed the two letters he received from King Djedkare of Dynasty 5 on the entrance to his mastaba at Giza. Similarly, after recording his repeated success at Yam to the south of Egypt, Harkhuf, an expedition leader buried at Aswan, inscribed on the facade of his rock tomb a copy of a letter he received from King Pepy II of Dynasty 6. The contents of the letter were of no great consequence, with the child king asking Harkhuf to

Pl. 17 Biographical inscriptions, Hesi, Saqqara, Dynasty 6

Pl. 18 Claims of moral goodness, Kaaper, Saqqara, Dynasty 6

take extra precautions for the safety of a pygmy whom he brought with him, and promising him unusual rewards in return. The main significance of the letter, he states, was that it was from the king himself and bears his own seal! From the New Kingdom Ahmose son of Ibana wrote a long biography in his tomb at El-Kab describing his acts of bravery and the rewards he received during the liberation wars against the Hyksos at the beginning of the Eighteenth Dynasty. In the reign of Thutmose III, the vizier Rekhmire inscribed in his tomb long texts outlining his career, the duties of his post and an installation speech given by the king who tells Rekhmire that the vizier is the pillar for the whole land and warns that the post is not sweet but bitter as gall. He then says:

Lo, petitioners come from the South and the North; the whole land is eager for the counsel of the vizier. See to it that all is done according to law, that all is done exactly right.

These biographical inscriptions seem to aim at impressing their readers, perhaps more so than the rather common and stereotyped claims of moral goodness, such as:

I gave bread to the hungry, beer to the thirsty and clothing to the naked. I carried out justice for its lord, and satisfied god with what he loves. I brought to land he who had no ferry-boat. I was one who said what was good and who reported what was good, ... (pl. 18).

The impressed reader was expected to present offerings, utter invocation offering formula, or perhaps simply remember and mention the name of the tomb owner.

Recording of Names

The desire that a man's name be remembered is recorded in a number of funerary inscriptions. For example, from the Late Period Djehutirekh wrote an address to the visitors of the necropolis:

> Oh you who are alive on earth, who shall come here to this desert; all who come to offer in this graveyard: pronounce my name with abundant libation, Thoth will favour you for it. It is rewarding to act for him who cannot act, ... I am a man whose name should be pronounced!

In a prayer to Amun, written on the statue of Montemhat, also from the Late Period, the owner says:

> May he put love of me in people's hearts, that everyone be fond of me. May he grant me a good burial in the graveyard of my city; the sacred land is in his grasp. May he make my name last like heaven's stars, my statue endure as one of his followers. May my Ka be remembered in his temple night and day. May I renew my youth like the moon. May my name not be forgotten in after years ever.

Close to the former in date, Petosiris built a family tomb in Hermopolis and clearly indicated in his biography the purpose of building the tomb as:

> I built this tomb in the necropolis, beside the great souls who are there, in order that my father's name be pronounced, and that of my elder brother. A man is revived when his name is pronounced!

The teachings written in the Insinger Papyrus explain the wisdom behind this desire to commemorate one's name as:

> The grace of the god for the man of god is his burial and his resting place. The renewal of life before the dying is leaving his name on earth behind him.

The Ramesside author of Papyrus Chester Beatty IV carries this theme much further by stating that immortality is more securely and permanently achieved not by building a solid tomb but by writing a book which would make the author's name live in the mouths of people. The author of the papyrus, obviously a writer himself, almost negates the value of all the preparations the Egyptians made for the

afterlife. Talking about the immortality of writers he says:

> They did not make for themselves tombs of copper, with stelae of metal from heaven. They knew not how to leave heirs, children of theirs to pronounce their names: they made heirs for themselves of books, of Instructions they had composed. They gave themselves the scroll as lector-priest, the writing-board as a loving son. Instructions are their tombs, the reed pen is their child, the stone-surface is their wife. People great and small are given them as children.

Then he states that:

> Better is a book than a graven stela, than a solid tomb-enclosure. They (i.e., books) act as chapels and tombs, in the heart of him who speaks their name. Surely useful in the graveyard is a name in people's mouths!

The author then lists some of the great sages of the past, Hardjedef, Imhotep, Neferti, Khety, etc. and states that they are not remembered because of their tombs, stelae, heirs or priests, but because of their writings.

From this survey of the evidence we can see that the Egyptian believed that in the life to come he needed sustenance both on earth and in the Netherworld. On earth, and particularly for those who could afford it, land and priests were set aside for this purpose, but he also appealed to his relatives, descendants and people in general for assistance in the form of offerings, invocation offerings or simply uttering his name. The Netherworld was a land of abundance but in order to receive a piece of this land to cultivate, the deceased's actions during his earthly life had first to be judged.

SADNESS AND SCEPTICISM

Although the Egyptian belief in perpetual life in the Hereafter should have produced optimism, at least among the classes which enjoyed more privileges, the picture one gets from the didactic literature is that they were generally not less grieved by, or less fearful of, death than any other people of any time. But like that of other cultures, the Egyptian outlook on death does not seem to have been uniform, nor did it remain unchanged throughout the different periods of their history.

A comparison of the Instruction of Prince Hardjedef with that addressed to King Merikare, clearly shows an ideological development which took place as early as the First Intermediate Period.

While both texts provide advice on tomb-building, the teaching of Merikare is more spiritual and ethical; it emphasises the need to build the funerary monument on righteousness and justice. In advising his son to build a tomb, Prince Hardjedef tells him that life exalts us and that death humbles us. This theme, however, does not seem to have been stressed in the literature of the Old Kingdom. On the other hand, .it was well developed in a number of literary works from the First Intermediate Period. Most relevant to the theme under discussion is a text usually called 'A dispute between a man and his Ba'. It portrays a man, for whom the evils of life were too burdensome, who sees in death a solution to his troubles. His Ba does not concur, and threatens to abandon him and thus deprive him of any hope in the Hereafter. The text, therefore, gives two views of death: one is that of the man, the other is that of his Ba. 'Just as trees fall, so is human life temporary', according to the man who does not want to pro'ong his misery. Death to him is:

> Like a sick man's recovery, like going into the open after confinement, ... like the fragrance of lotus blossoms, like sitting on the bank of drunkenness, ... like a man's coming home from warfare, ... like the longing of a man to see his home after he has spent many years in captivity.

His Ba on the other hand reminds him that:

> If you think of burial, it is heartbreak. It is the bringing of tears and the cause of grief for a man. It is taking a man from his house and casting him on the hillside. You will never come up to see the sun.

His Ba even seems sceptical about the worth of building tombs since

> Those who built in granite, who erected halls in excellent tombs of excellent construction, when the builders have become gods (i.e., died), their offering-stones are desolate, as if they were the dead who died on the riverbank for lack of a survivor.

Pl. 19 (top) Mourning, Ankhmahor, Saqqara, Dynasty 6
Pl. 20 (bottom) Mourning, Ramose, Thebes, Dynasty 18

47

The text is set in such a way that the tone of the Ba's words is particularly surprising, for while the man understandably sees in death a sweet end, a deliverance from all his pains, the Ba seems to talk objectively and realistically, emphasising that life is worth living and that those who built rich tombs are ultimately no better off than those who did not. Also, although the Ba does not succeed in persuading the man not to take his life, the tone of scepticism is registered very strongly.

Contradictory Views

The conflict between the two viewpoints concerning death and the futility of tomb-building continued throughout Egyptian history and is well represented in a group of songs usually entitled 'the Harpists' Songs'. These appear to have originated in the Middle Kingdom, although the copies we have were written on papyri or in tombs dating from the New Kingdom. The following excerpts from two of these songs demonstrate the contradictions in their approach. In one song the harpist says:

> Those who build tombs, their places are gone. See, what has been made of them? I have heard the words of Imhotep and Hardjedef, whose sayings men recite so much. What are their places now? Their walls have crumbled, their places have gone, as though they had never been. No one returns from there, that he may tell of their state, that he may tell of their needs, that he may calm our hearts until we go where they have gone.

The singer then invites people to enjoy the pleasures of life while they can, until that day of mourning comes:

> Follow your heart while you live, put myrrh on your head, clothe yourself with fine linen ... Make your things on earth, do not destroy your heart, until that day of lamentation comes for you!'

He also reminds people that 'wailing cannot save a man from the tomb-pit', that 'no one is allowed to take his property with him', and that 'no one who departs returns again'.
In the other song the harpist, possibly being aware of the above song, says:

> I have heard those songs which are in the ancient tombs, and what they tell in praising life on earth, and in belittling the land of the dead. Why is this done to the land of eternity, the right and just, that has no terrors? Strife is abhorrent to it, and no one arrays himself against his fellow ... As to the time of deeds on earth, it is the passing of a dream. One says: "Welcome safe and sound", to him who reaches the West.

The singer reminds people that all ancestors and all successors will be resting in the land of the dead, for 'no one may linger in the land of Egypt'.

Such contradictory ideas are curious and must have resulted from practical observation by the Egyptian of what had become of the ancestors' tombs, and subsequently his deep questioning of his funerary beliefs and practices, perhaps at certain difficult times more than others. It is even more astonishing that such conflicting ideology could sometimes exist side by side in one and the same tomb.

The peak of scepticism may however be found, as seen above, in papyrus Chester Beatty IV, a Ramesside text setting out the advantage of learning and the immortality of writings and writers. So far, in Egyptian thought, doubt had been cast on the durability of tombs and the uncertainty of the nature of life in the Hereafter. But here for the first time the author negates the practicality and therefore the logic behind preserving the body in order to have a perpetual life:

> A man decays, his corpse is dust, all his relatives have perished, but it is writing that makes him remembered through the mouth of the reciter. More effective is a book than a well-built house or a tomb in the west.

Scepticism continued in the Late Period and in the Ptolemaic times. Sishu, for example, informs us that he did everything good and pure on earth, but he advises the living to drink till they are drunk, to enjoy their moment on earth and make use of their goods, for 'when a man departs his goods depart, he who inherits them does his wish in turn'. We find the same idea in the long instructions written on the Insinger Papyrus:

> The end of the devout man will be buried on the hillside with his burial equipment. The owner of millions who acquired them by hoarding cannot take them to the hillside in his hand.

The same author advises:

> Do not prefer death to life in misfortune out of despair. God returns contentment, the dead do not return.

Fear of Death

Sorrow and fear of death is a constant refrain in these periods. Taimhotep, who was born under Ptolemy XII and died under Cleopatra VII at the age of thirty, had a stela made for her by her husband, where she mourns her premature death and advises her husband:

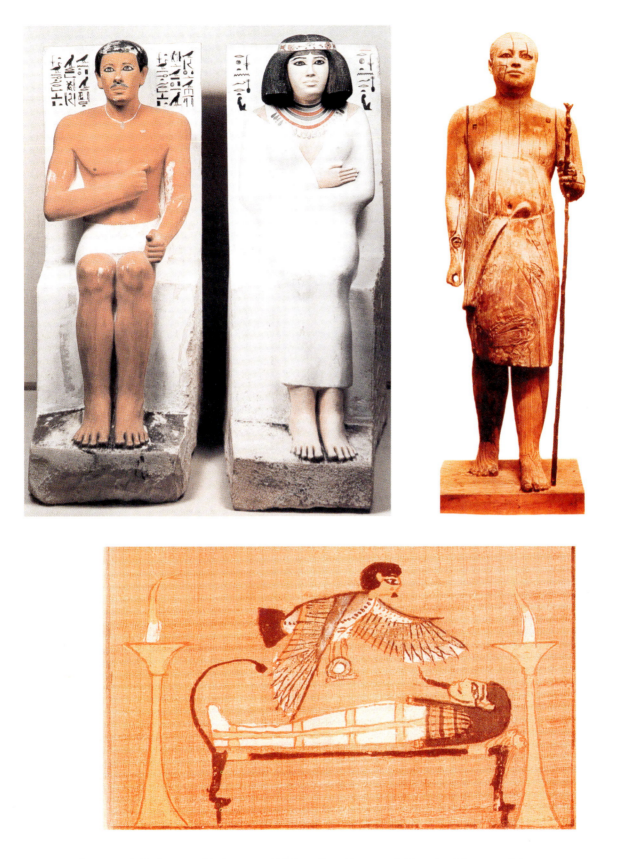

Pl. 21 (top left) Statues of Rahotep and Nefert, Giza, Dynasty 4, Egyptian Museum, Cairo
Pl. 22 (top right) Wooden statue of Kaaper (Sheik el-Balad), Dynasty 5, Egyptian Museum, Cairo
Pl. 23 (bottom) The Ba hovers over its mummy, Papyrus Any, Dynasty 19, British Museum

Pl. 24 (top) Canopic jars, Dynasty 21, British Museum
Pl. 25 (centre) At the gate of the tomb, Papyrus Any, Dynasty 19, British Museum
Pl. 26 (bottom) Funeral procession, Papyrus Any, Dynasty 19, British Museum

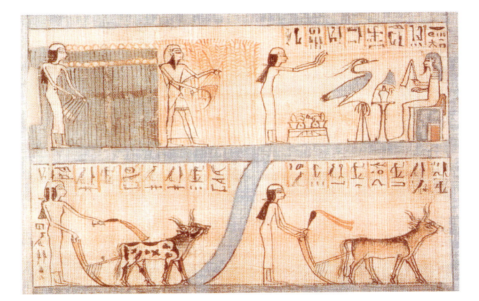

Pl. 27 (top) The Opening of the Mouth ceremony, Nebamun and Ipuky, Thebes, Dynasty 18
Pl. 28 (centre) Anhai and her husband in the Field of Reeds, papyrus, Dynasty 20, British Museum
Pl. 29 (bottom) At the gate in the Netherworld, Sennedjem, Thebes, Dynasty 19

Pl. 30 (top) Tomb owner in the Netherworld, Sennedjem, Thebes, Dynasty 19
Pl. 31 (bottom) Judgement of the deceased, Papyrus Any, Dynasty 19, British Museum

Value the years spent on earth! The west, it is a land of sleep, darkness weighs on the dwelling-place, those who are there sleep in their mummy-forms. They wake not to see their brothers, they see not their fathers, their mothers, their hearts forget their wives, their children.

She also says that death does not distinguish between the young and old and that everyone is afraid of it:

He snatches the son from his mother, before the old man who walks by his side. Frightened, they all plead before him, but he turns not his ear to them.

The reaction of people in general, and relatives in particular, to the passing away of a person may be seen in Neferti's disappointment over the apathetic attitude towards death which he had encountered. Describing a period of disorder in the Middle Kingdom, Neferti says:

No one will weep over death, no one will spend the night fasting because of death; each man's heart is for himself. Mourning is not carried out today, for hearts have completely abandoned it.

In the Late Period Nebnetjeru says that everybody grieved for his death:

How the land mourned when I passed away, the people no less than my kin.

The mourning of the dead is vividly depicted in many scenes from ancient Egypt, with little variation in the expression of grief in different periods (pls. 19, 20). These scenes give the same picture we get from the description of Egyptian mourning customs given by the Greek historian of the Fifth Century BC, Herodotus, who says that relatives smeared their heads and faces with mud and beat themselves. Scenes also show relatives collapsing to the ground, tearing their hair and clothes in a desperate state of grief. The same customs have survived among the Egyptian village communities of today.

With such a sad and sceptical attitude towards death, it is not strange to find that old age was particularly valued since it afforded more years on earth. Long life was considered as a divine gift, and was frequently recorded in biographical inscriptions.

Thus the magician Djedi in the Tale of Wonder is said to be one hundred and ten years old, the same age as the sage Ptahhotep who graphically described the difficulties brought about by old age:

Feebleness came, weakness grows, childlike one sleeps all day. Eyes are dim, ears deaf, strength is waning through weariness. The mouth, silenced, speaks not. The heart, void, recalls not the past. The bones ache throughout. Good has become evil, all taste is gone. What age does to people is evil in everything. The nose, clogged, breathes not. Painful are standing and sitting.

Despite its problems old age was appreciated and Ptahhotep who was writing for his son wishes it for him: 'May you obtain many years of life'. Pepyankh-heryib of Meir recorded his hundredth year, presumably the same age attained by King Pepy II under whom he served. Nebnetjeru, from the Late Period, records that he 'attained the age of ninety-six, being healthy, without sickness'.

It follows that death at an early age was considered particularly sad, and the Hereafter in such cases was described as the land of deprivation, the land of thirst and darkness which had deprived the deceased from enjoying all the pleasures of a full life on earth. Two inscriptions belonging to deceased can throw light on the Egyptian view of premature death. Djehutirekh says:

Who hears my speech, his heart will grieve for it, for I am a small child snatched by force, abridged in years as an innocent one, snatched quickly as a little one, like a man carried off by sleep. I was a youngster of ... years, when taken to the city of eternity, ..., without having my share. I was rich in friends. All the men of my town, not one of them could protect me! ... All my friends mourned for me, father and mother implored death, my brothers, they mourned since I reached this land of deprivation.

Isenkhebe also says:

I lie in the vale, a young girl, I thirst with water beside me. I was driven from childhood too early, turned away from my house as a youngster, before I had my fill in it. The dark, a child's terror, engulfed me, while the breast was in my mouth. The demons of this hall bar everyone from me, I am too young to be alone!

53

II: Tomb Architecture

THE EARLIEST GRAVES

As man dwelt in a house during his lifetime, so he needed an abode for his body in the afterlife. The idea of constructing a tomb developed as soon as the Egyptian settled in the Nile Valley and built a house, and the general shape of the tomb was probably influenced by that of his house. It should be emphasised, however, that one can speak only broadly of the architectural features of each period; elements typical for one period may well have appeared earlier and continued in use for some time after. Furthermore, a general work such as the present one is restricted to basic developments without discussing the finer details.

Although the early settlers, the Badarians (around 4500-3800 BC), appear to have attempted to dig rectangular graves for their dead, the vast majority of their burials were in shallow, roughly circular or oval shaped pits. Their form was probably dictated by the nature of the sandy soil of the desert, the simple tools (potsherds may have been used for digging), and the lack of lining to help the walls of the grave retain their shape. In some instances sticks were found in graves, but whether these were used for lining is doubtful. Similarly, branches were discovered which might have supported a roof, but no evidence of a superstructure above this was ever found, although this could have been a small heap of sand. In certain cemeteries the female graves are larger than those of the male; in others the opposite is true. The size of a grave surely reflects the importance of its occupant, but, since no complete records of the owners' sexes have been kept for many excavated sites, any attempt to study the relative status of men and women, or the chronological development of their graves, is only tentative with our present knowledge.

The deceased was already laid in the position which was to become characteristic of the Predynastic Period in Upper Egypt (4500-3050 BC), a contracted position on the left side facing west, with the hands clenched near the face and the head towards the south (see fig. 1). The body was frequently wrapped in a mat or in a hide for protection, and some provisions were placed either outside this wrapping or in a small niche dug in one of the walls of the grave. Funerary provisions were simple, a pot, a cosmetic slate palette, a necklace of stone beads and shells and frequently flint implements. The position of the body in the grave

may simply represent that of sleep, yet its consistency, the direction of the face to the west where the sun sets, and the presence of funerary provisions may suggest some religious significance. The burial position may, therefore, be likened to that of a foetus, in preparation for rebirth in the afterlife. The absence of writing in the Predynastic Period makes the interpretation of the funerary beliefs of the time difficult, but the consistency of the evidence obtained from the graves is significant.

There is no noticeable development in the shape of graves between those of the Badarians and of their successors or part contemporaries in Naqada I (4000-3600 BC); the dating in each case relies on the type of funerary furnishings (pottery, amulets, flint knives, etc.) characteristic of the period. The graves of Naqada II (3600-3200 BC), on the other hand, show a deliberate attempt to achieve a rectangular shape for the pits, either by lining the walls with basketwork or mats and sticks, or by plastering the walls of the grave with mud. Sticks and matting, and very rarely wooden planks, were used for roofing. These new developments restricted the possibility of cutting a niche, which had to be placed above the lining. In the majority of cases, however, the ever-increasing funerary furnishings were put inside the grave, which then had to be enlarged, or were placed between the wooden frame and the walls of the grave. In the latter part of the Naqada II Period, a new feature appeared: a larger niche was cut with its floor at a level lower than that of the pit floor, and the body itself was pushed inside it. Burial pits were lined with wooden planks or mud plaster, but instances of mud-brick lining are also known. Mud-brick or mud and rubble were similarly used for the construction of houses and grain kilns, which now tended to become rectangular. The development of the rectangular tomb should not alone be taken as an indication of a later date, as the shape might have been influenced by the means of its owner and by whether he was a town resident or a village dweller. At Naqada some graves were dug into the floor of houses. However, during the Naqada III phase (3200-3050 BC), the edge of the desert was regularly used for burials. A study of the evidence from Predynastic graves suggests a gradual increase in social hierarchy and socio-political organisation.

THE OLD KINGDOM MASTABAS

During the Archaic period, because of the new wealth resulting from the unification of the country, tombs of the rich grew larger and more storage areas were provided for funerary goods. This was achieved by building above the grave a mud-brick superstructure containing a large number of magazines. These superstructures were frequently decorated in the First Dynasty on one or more of their exterior faces with the so-called palace-façade panelling (fig. 30). The grave itself, i.e., the substructure, was now cut into the rock level under the superstructure and often roofed with wooden planks. It also contained some storerooms in addition to the burial chamber and from the middle of the First Dynasty, perhaps to provide better security, the trend was to decrease the number of magazines in the superstructure and to increase the storerooms in the substructure. This grew deeper, and by Dynasty 2 had become a long passage with side chambers opening off a central corridor, with a stairway providing access (fig. 31). The superstructure, on the other hand, became a solid, rectangular block with retaining walls and a core of sand and rubble. In the eastern façade two offering niches were built into the brickwork, probably to replace the earlier exterior panelling, and to later be replaced by false doors made of stone. Tombs of lower officials followed the same development but were generally smaller, while those of the majority of the population presumably continued the Predynastic style, with the body wrapped in matting, animal skin or cloth and placed in an oval or rectangular pit. Others lined the pit with mud-bricks.

Grave goods became varied during the Archaic Period and included stone vessels, copper vessels, jewellery, wooden furniture, games, tools and, above all, provisions of food and drink - bread loaves, cuts of meat and beverages such as wine and beer. The burial of wooden boats near some elite tombs at Saqqara and Helwan for example suggests that a belief in a celestial journey already existed. The Second Dynasty tombs at Helwan included also stone stelae (wrongly called ceiling stelae) recording the name and titles of the owner and depicting him/her usually at an offering table. It was also during this period that large slabs of stone were used, as evident at Helwan, in lining and roofing the burial chambers and for blocking the entrance stairways at intervals with portcullises.

The Mastaba

A tomb with a constructed superstructure, originally of mud-brick and later also of stone, is usually called a mastaba. The name was given to these tombs by the Egyptian workmen of the early French archaeologist Mariette, who saw a resemblance between these constructions and the bench-like seats, usually made of mud-brick, found in front of peasants' houses and called in Arabic 'mastabas'.

The architecture of the mastabas underwent constant development, but the change proceeded faster in the Memphite tombs than in those of Upper Egypt, and in the tombs of the rich than in those of the poor. The stairway entrance to the substructure was gradually replaced by a deep, vertical shaft or less commonly a sloping passage, mostly in the rock-cut tombs in the provinces, but also at Meydum. The subterranean rooms were reduced in most cases to one relatively large burial chamber. As for the superstructure, brick walls were built around the offering niches in order to protect them, creating simple exterior chapels (fig. 32). (The term chapel is usually given to the one or more rooms in the superstructure of a tomb where the funerary rites of the deceased were maintained and offerings were presented.) Alternatively, a wall was built in front of the eastern façade, creating a corridor chapel which contained the offering niches (fig. 33). In other instances these niches, particularly the southern one, were moved inside the superstructure, forming what is called a cruciform chapel (fig. 34).

The southern offering niche, usually larger than the northern and considered the more important, was reserved for the tomb owner, while the northern one was for his wife. This was the case in all sites as far south as El-Kab. At Edfu, on the other hand, the northern niche was the most important. This may

Fig. 30 Plan of palace façade panelling

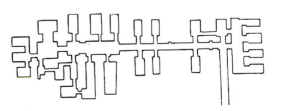

Fig. 31 Plan of the substructure of a Second Dynasty tomb

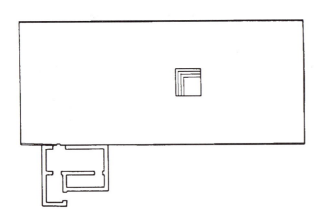

Fig. 32 Plan of a stone mastaba with exterior chapel and one shaft

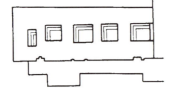

Fig. 33 Plan of a mastaba with corridor chapel

Fig. 34 Plan of a cruciform chapel

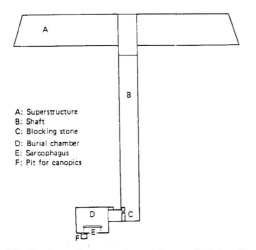

A: Superstructure
B: Shaft
C: Blocking stone
D: Burial chamber
E: Sarcophagus
F: Pit for canopics

Fig. 35 Section of a mastaba with one shaft leading to a burial chamber

suggest that the mastabas of the Old Kingdom were orientated towards a point south of El-Kab and north of Edfu, a location which would suit the oldest known sanctuary of Hierakonpolis.

The three above-mentioned types of chapels (exterior chapel, corridor chapel and cruciform chapel) appeared sporadically at the end of the Archaic Period, becoming common by the beginning of Dynasty 4. Mud-brick was the main building material, although large stone slabs were employed in some instances. By the reign of Khufu, the use of stone became more common, particularly for the tombs of the rich. Streets of limestone mastabas were constructed for Khufu's officials around his great pyramid at Giza. The shafts were excavated into the bedrock before the mastaba was built, with their walls above ground level constructed of mud-brick or stone within the core of the mastaba, so that access to the shaft was from the top of the mastaba (fig. 35).

The depth of the shaft varied in accordance with different periods and the wealth of the owner since depth represented the best protection for the contents of the burial chamber. The main shaft of a vizier's tomb in the Teti cemetery, for example, was approximately twenty metres deep. At the bottom of the shaft the burial chamber opened to the west and often extended to the south. Another type of substructure, more costly and accordingly less popular, was formed by digging a trench in which a sloping passage and a burial chamber were constructed of stone. Examples of this type are found in the Fourth Dynasty tombs at Meydum. In all types however, every effort was made to locate the subterranean burial chambers within the perimeter of the mastaba itself. As the cemetery was designed like a city with streets, and plots of different sizes and locations in relation to the reigning king's pyramid were allocated to individuals according to their status, such care in locating the burial chamber was essential in order to avoid tomb owners breaking into each others' burial chambers. With the later growth of cemeteries however, such accidents became the norm. A canopic chest holding the viscera of the deceased was placed in the burial chamber, either in a pit, with a stone lid, excavated in the south-east corner, or in a niche cut into the south wall or into the southern end of the east wall. A larger pit or a niche, contiguous with the west wall of the burial chamber, was often cut to accommodate a large stone sarcophagus. This was usually formed of two blocks, one for the chest and another for the lid, which were certainly lowered into the chamber before the walls of the superstructure were built. In Dynasties 5 and 6 the pit was sometimes provided with a lid and replaced the sarcophagus itself. The burial chamber was blocked following interment with a thin wall of masonry, mud-brick or rough stone. A blocking slab of stone was sometimes lowered in front of the entrance to the chamber. The shaft was then filled with debris which probably resulted from its original cutting. But all of these precautions and many more ingenious techniques developed in later periods to prevent tomb robbery were in vain, for hardly any burial chamber containing valuable funerary goods escaped the attention of robbers.

By the beginning of the Fifth Dynasty interior chapels became common, although these were still small in relation to the total area of the mastabas, which were constructed of solid masonry or of stone or of mud-brick retaining walls with rubble cores (fig. 36). The older types of chapels - the cruciform and the short corridor - continued to be built, but new types also appeared. Popular were the L-shaped

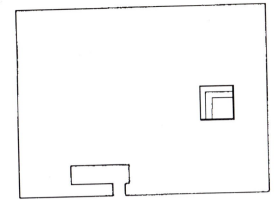

Fig. 36 Plan of mastaba with L-shaped chapel and one shaft

chapels and the east-west offering chambers, the latter continuing in use until the end of Dynasty 6. Characteristic of tombs of wealthy high officials at the end of Dynasty 5 and the beginning of Dynasty 6, the peak of Old Kingdom art and architecture,

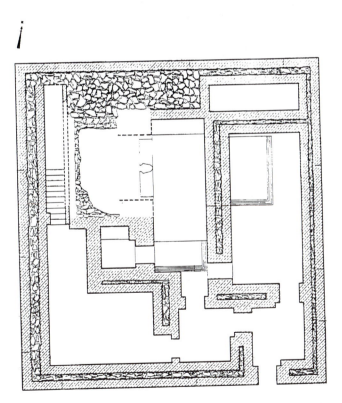

Fig. 37 Plan of the mastaba of Nikauisesi, Saqqara, Dynasty 6

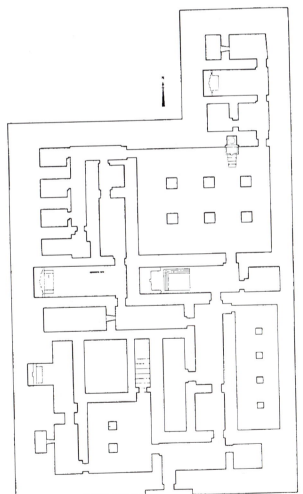

Fig. 38 Plan of the mastaba of Mereruka, Saqqara, Dynasty 6

57

were the complex interior chapels with several rooms, pillared halls and pillared porticos, which often occupied the entire area of the mastabas. Examples of this type are found in the tombs of Ti, Ptahhotep, Mereruka, Nikauisesi and Khentika at Saqqara (figs. 37, 38). With the entire area of the mastaba occupied by rooms, the mouths of all shafts now opened into the floors of these rooms. Complex interior chapels continued to be built with mud-brick, as for example in the case of Kaaper in the Teti cemetery. However, in these cases chapels had to be constructed as a series of small, or corridor-like, rooms to allow for the construction of vaulted roofs. No such restriction was needed for stone-built chapels, as it was possible to roof large rooms by dividing them longitudinally with rows of pillars carrying architraves, thus allowing shorter roofing slabs to be used.

This increase in the number of rooms in the chapel expanded the wall surface available for decoration, and in turn resulted in a larger and richer repertoire of scenes. The decoration of burial chambers also began in this period but remained exclusive to the top officials such as viziers. The number of shafts in each mastaba generally increased, yet it is curious that there is no correlation between the size of the mastaba and the number of shafts it contains, some of the largest mastabas, for example that of Neferseshemre in the Teti cemetery, has only one shaft. The number of shafts in the tomb presumably depended on the number of family members who did not possess independent tombs. As the owners of the largest mastabas were not only rich, but also influential, their children were guaranteed offices, usually in the same administrative area as their fathers, and accordingly built their own tombs. Married daughters were buried in their husbands' tombs. Many rich tomb owners, whilst depicting their children in their chapels, did not represent a wife nor was a special shaft prepared for her. In such cases one may assume that by the time these officials constructed their tombs their wives were either divorced or already dead and buried elsewhere. Access to the shafts was now provided from the floor of various rooms of the chapel rather than from the top of the mastaba. However, if the chapel did not occupy the total area of the mastaba, shafts were sometimes still positioned in its solid part, with their mouths opening from the terrace on top of the mastaba, as is the case in the tombs of Ankhmahor and Neferseshemre near Teti's pyramid at Saqqara. The plan of these mastabas parallels that of a typical house of the period, with an entrance area, reception rooms, magazines and residential apartments, as well as an internal staircase rising from an open court, as in the mastaba of Nikauisesi, or from a pillared hall to the terrace of the mastaba. However, a study of the positioning of the pillars suggests that many of these halls, such as that of Ankhmahor, were only partly roofed with the other part open to the sky. It was by this staircase that the funeral procession reached the often walled terrace, where rites were performed before the mummy was lowered down the shaft. The false door of Neferseshemre records a meal celebrated near the mouth of the shaft before the burial took place.

False Doors

The most important architectural element, and one which is found in almost all decorated tombs, is the so-called false door, or Ka-door (fig. 10, pl. 4). Made rarely of wood, as in the case of Hesire, but more frequently of a monolithic piece of good quality limestone which was often painted red with black spots probably to imitate granite, as in the case of Seankhuiptah in the Teti cemetery, the false door is not a copy of a real door, but it is a combination of the offering niche and the stela with an offering table scene, both common during the first two dynasties. Thus, like the offering niche, the false door possesses one, two or three pairs of jambs, leading to a central niche. Above the niche is a rounded element, usually called a drum, which probably represents a rolled-up woven curtain. A lintel extends across the jambs, above which is a panel on which is usually represented the tomb owner at an offering table. A pair of outer jambs

Pl. 32 False door and offering slab, Hesi, Saqqara, Dynasty 6

and an architrave form a frame around the door. About the middle of Dynasty 5 two new features were added to the false door and became characteristic of later examples. These are the torus moulding and the cavetto cornice, both elements deriving from a door constructed of plants and representing a frame bound with fibre and a palm cornice (figs. 3, 10).

The name 'false door' was given to this architectural feature by scholars because, while the spiritual entities of the deceased were believed to have the ability to pass through the door, this did not open or close. However, the Third Dynasty door of Hesire was probably furnished with moveable wooden panels, as were possibly some of the early offering niches. Most of the elements of the false door are usually inscribed with the name and titles of the owner, often with the addition of his figure. A few doors also have a statue of the owner in the central niche, and that of Neferseshemptah in the Teti cemetery possesses one standing statue in each of its outer jambs and a bust statue in the central panel instead of the offering table scene (pl. 14). The west wall of the main room in the chapel, the offering chamber, is the most common location of the false door. Its presence is intended to guide the deceased's spiritual entities to his burial chamber, which is usually positioned beneath the door and is reached by a shaft found in front of or behind the door. If two false doors are fixed to the west wall, customarily the southern one is allocated to the tomb owner and the northern one to his wife. But some mastabas possess several false doors, one for each member of the family buried there, usually located near the shaft leading to its respective burial chamber. In front of each false door was an offering slab in *hetep* shape (a loaf-on-mat sign) on which food and drink were placed for the Ka (pls. 15, 32). These are made of good quality stone and frequently include a number of depressions used as dishes and basins and regularly depict in relief a loaf of bread and occasionally other items such as a goose, an ox head, etc. Actual offerings were certainly placed on the *hetep*-slab at least for some time, since an examination of some of these, for example those of

Nikauisesi and Shepsipuptah in the Teti cemetery, shows that the stone in the area of the loaf-sign is badly worn, while the rest of the slab, usually made of a good, compact piece of limestone, is in an excellent state of preservation. The offerings placed there were later redistributed among priests and necropolis workers. Among the food favoured by the Egyptians was meat and it seems that animals were slaughtered in the chapel. Tethering stones for tying up sacrificial animals are fixed into the floor of certain chapels, as in that of Mereruka, and tethering holes are pierced in the walls and various door thicknesses of others, such as Nikauisesi's mastaba.

Serdabs

Another architectural element found in many mastabas is the so-called serdab, which in Arabic means cellar. The serdab is a room within the retaining walls of the mastaba in which one or more statues of the tomb owner, and sometimes of members of his family or household, were concealed for safety. Situated near the chapel, the serdab is linked to this room only by apertures cut into the masonry between them (fig. 39). As the Ka was believed to be capable of dwelling in a statue of its owner, placing such an image in a sealed serdab was a safeguard against the possible decay or destruction of the mummy. Through the apertures of the serdab the Ka could find its statues and could then observe the scenes depicted in the chapel, the visiting relatives, the rites performed by priests, and the offerings presented. Some mastabas possess a number of serdabs which must have enclosed many statues of their owners and relations.

THE OLD KINGDOM ROCK-CUT TOMBS

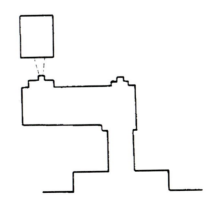

Fig. 39 Plan of L-shaped chapel with two false doors and a serdab.

Pl. 33 Pillared-hall in a mastaba, Mereruka, Saqqara, Dynasty 6

Pl. 34 Pillared-hall in a rock-cut tomb, Sarenput II, Aswan, Dynasty 12

Pl. 35 Rock-cut mastaba, Minankh, El-Hawawish, Dynasty 5

The earliest rock tombs are found at Giza. These are cut into the terraces created as a result of the quarrying of stone from the Giza plateau for the construction of the pyramids. A few rock tombs (or tombs partly cut into the rock and partly built of stone) exist also at Saqqara but the vast majority of this type of tomb is found in the various Upper Egyptian provinces, where an ideal setting is provided by the cliffs at the edge of the deserts on both sides of the Nile valley (see pl. 3). It should be emphasised that the rock tombs were never considered inferior to mastabas, and perhaps were even preferred. Not only were the rock tombs more durable - an advantage which could not have escaped the observation of the practical Egyptian - but also the earliest rock tombs were assigned to queens and members of the royal family of Khafre, rather than to ordinary officials. If the dignitaries of the country continued to build mastabas, it was probably because of the geographical features of the capital cemeteries and/or the desire to be buried in the immediate vicinity of either the royal pyramid or other members of the tomb owner's family. In the Upper Egyptian provinces, on the other hand, officials chose to cut their tombs in the nearby mountains as early as the Fourth Dynasty at Tehna near the modern town of Minya. However, the burials of officials in the provinces did not become common until the end of the Fifth Dynasty. The cutting of rock tombs continued during the Middle Kingdom, and in the New Kingdom even the kings and the royal family preferred to place their tombs in the cliffs on the west bank at Thebes. In the Delta where no cliffs are present officials used the available material, the Nile silt, to build their tombs with mud-brick, although some used limestone blocks, brought from faraway quarries, to line the walls of their burial chambers. Most of the Delta cemeteries are now covered by silt deposit and are difficult to excavate. Some, however, have been cleared at Tell el-Rubaa. Mud-brick was also used to build tombs in the Oases, such as Dakhla.

The rock-cut tomb should not be thought of as a later development superseding the mastaba, for the construction of the two types continued simultaneously at different sites. Thus while Upper Egyptian officials in most provinces cut their tombs in the nearest hill near their town, those with no suitable cliffs in their vicinity built mastabas, as for example at Edfu and Dendera. At Deshasha, two known governors cut tombs in very low cliffs, while a third opted to build a mastaba. Governed by the same funerary beliefs, the architectural features of both types of tomb were basically very similar: a public area, i.e., a chapel composed of one or more rooms, an offering area in which was placed the tomb owner's false door, a serdab for statues, a magazine(s) for storing food items etc., as well as a substructure consisting of shafts and burial chambers. Furthermore, as most of the distinguished individuals of the Old Kingdom constructed mastabas at Giza and Saqqara, certain architectural elements introduced for mastabas were copied by provincial officials in their rock-cut tombs, even though these elements were unnecessary for this type of architecture. An obvious example of such imitation is the use of pillars and architraves in both types of tombs. In mastabas, rows of pillars carrying architraves were added to large halls so that stone slabs of reasonable length could be used for roofing. No such elements were necessary in the case of rock-hewn halls, yet they were commonly employed (pls. 33, 34). In both mastabas and rock-cut tombs some architects painted the roofs in red with black spots to give the impression of red granite being used as roofing slabs. Some officials even went further by isolating a piece of rock on the mountain, and shaping it in the form of a mastaba, even with slanting exterior sides, in which they cut their chapel. This type of tomb, as in the case of Nikaankh of Tehna and Minankh of El-Hawawish, may be called a rock-cut mastaba (pl. 35).

Unlike mastabas, rock-cut tombs required no special pieces of stone to be provided for the various architectural elements. Thus pillars, architraves, false doors, offering slabs, etc., were usually formed in the native rock during the cutting of the tomb. If this rock was of poor quality, it was covered with a layer of plaster or, less frequently, cased with better quality stone, before being decorated with scenes and inscriptions.

The cutting of the chapel into the cliffs reduced the problems of roofing and probably led the Egyptian to produce a large, single room instead of a multi-roomed chapel. Columned porticoes continued to be left in front of the chapel. The chapel of Hem-Min of Akhmim, from early Dynasty 6, measures 20.20 x 9.20 metres (fig. 40). Its ceiling, which is 3.90 metres high, was originally supported by two rows of pillars. Three pillars are now preserved in each row, although it is likely that six pillars were originally planned for each row. As the builders progressed in their cutting inside the mountain, they were faced with the gradual deteriorating quality of the rock, until no standing pillars were able to be shaped in the inner half. The pillars in the outer half are now mostly broken, yet the unsupported ceiling of the chapel remains for, as

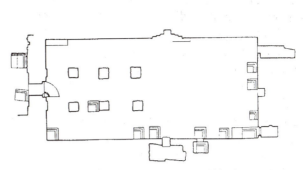

Fig. 40 *Plan of the tomb of Hem-Min, Akhmim, Dynasty 6*

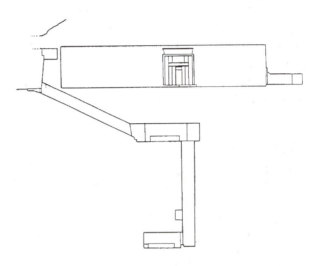

Fig. 41 *Section of the tomb of Hem-Min, showing the chapel and the two burial chambers at different levels, Akhmim, Dynasty 6*

Pl. 36 *Broken pillars, Hem-Min, El-Hawawish, Dynasty 6*

stated above, pillars in most rock tombs are superfluous and in direct imitation of the mastaba architecture (pl. 36).

Rock-cut chapels, on the other hand, produced a problem with the serdab. Since this is essentially a sealed room for statues, it was impossible to create without building a wall of masonry to block the serdab after it was cut into the mountain and the statues were placed in it. An alternative method, which equally guaranteed the safety of the statues in rock tombs, was preferred from the outset: statues were cut into the native rock, with their backs left attached to the wall. The tombs of Qar, Idu and Kaherptah at Giza, Irukaptah at Saqqara, Meru at Sheikh Said and Memi at Akhmim contain examples of these engaged statues (pl. 6). The number of the statues varies from one tomb to another, with the last-mentioned tomb containing 24 statues, and that of Kaherptah containing 29.

Tomb Robbery

Access to the burial chamber was either through a vertical shaft or a sloping passage, although in some instances the architects introduced an original design, no doubt with the purpose of misleading tomb robbers. In the above-mentioned tomb of Hem-Min at Akhmim, a sloping passage, 10 metres long, leads to a finished burial chamber which has a burial pit cut into the native rock to replace a sarcophagus (fig. 41). All features lead to the assumption that this was the final resting place of the owner. Astonishingly, a vertical shaft opens in a corner of this room and descends a further 10 metres, leading to the true burial chamber of Hem-Min, which is also provided with a burial pit. Three other high-ranking officials in the same province followed this unusual design before it was abandoned. The vertical shaft which opens into the floor of the upper burial chamber was perfectly sealed after the burial took place, in order not to be distinguished from the floor of the chamber. Finding the first chamber empty, it was hoped, would lead thieves to believe that the tomb was already robbed and to abandon their efforts. The precautions were in vain, for none of these tombs remained unviolated.

When the upper burial chamber of Hem-Min was cleared a thin crack forming a square shape was noticed in its floor. When examined, this appeared to be a perfectly square slab of limestone cut from the same mountain and used to plug the mouth of the vertical shaft, with plaster made from the same limestone filling the remaining gaps. When the plugging stone was removed, the filling of the vertical shaft, which was 10 metres deep, proved to be clean, unpolluted limestone rubble, at the end of which was a still-sealed burial chamber. All indications suggested that the burial chamber was undisturbed, yet when opened, this was found empty. The only logical conclusion is that the contents of the chamber, including the mummy, were robbed on the night after the burial, when the chamber was sealed but the shaft was not yet completely filled. Access to the burial chamber would have then been relatively simple, particularly with the co-operation of the necropolis workers, who were no doubt able to quickly seal the chamber once more. The unsuspecting members of the tomb owner's family would then resume filling of the shaft the next day. The examination of the subterranean chambers of any cemetery reveals tunnels excavated by tomb robbers connecting burial chambers in a straight line between the nearest two points. Only people with complete knowledge of the architectural features of these tombs would have been able to successfully determine the direction of these tunnels. That tomb robbery took place immediately after the burial may also be gathered from the mastaba of Nikauisesi at Saqqara. There, a small hole was made into the wall of the sarcophagus, the deceased's head was extracted and placed on top of the sarcophagus lid and presumably a collar and perhaps other jewellery were taken. There is no evidence that Nikauisesi's body was mummified; and since the parts found on top of the sarcophagus lid include the skull as well as all the vertebrae of the neck, the robbery must have taken place before the body deteriorated and when the head and neck were still attached by soft tissue. Breaking the neck would not only facilitate the removal of a collar, but more importantly would eliminate the deceased's power to revenge. Other tomb robbers removed the body, as for example in the case of Hem-Min of Akhmim, and presumably destroyed it.

Finally, it should be emphasised that the architecture of mastabas and rock tombs in the Old Kingdom shows great individuality and variety of design, and that it is difficult to speak of a characteristic tomb plan such as is found in later periods. As certain designs appeared at certain times within the Old Kingdom, the architectural features can be used to narrow the date assigned to a tomb. For example, the growing proportion of the area occupied by rooms in relation to the area of the mastaba is indicative of a date from the beginning of the Fifth Dynasty to the beginning of the Sixth. A false door with a torus moulding and a cavetto cornice is indicative of a date in the latter part of the Fifth Dynasty or later. During the Fifth Dynasty the usual orientation of the offering room was north-south, which changed to east-west early in Teti's reign. Towards the end of the same reign both orientations were used. Staircases leading to the mastaba's roof are characteristic of late Dynasty 5 to early Dynasty 6 (fig. 37).

FROM THE FIRST TO THE SECOND INTERMEDIATE PERIOD

The First Intermediate Period

The fall of the Old Kingdom, and the relatively unstable period which ensued, usually called the First Intermediate Period, brought also a decline in all forms of art and architecture in the country. The collapse of the central government at Memphis, with all its financial resources and bureaucratic organisation, deprived the artists and architects of the period of their main sponsors and clientèle. Hence, the main schools of art in the capital, which no doubt also had a very strong influence on other centres in Egypt, lost their very reason for existence. Social unrest, internal fighting between different parts of the country, and severe famines must also have adversely affected all art forms.

It is true that certain provincial governors of the time tried to maintain a façade of normality and to claim absolute control of the situation in their provinces in Upper Egypt; but these are isolated cases, and their claims are probably exaggerated. On the other hand, the lot of many other Upper Egyptian noble families was tied to that of their sovereigns, and with the collapse of the royal house at Memphis they also disappeared. The few who succeeded in continuing to govern their provinces attempted to impress their contemporaries by building large tombs, but these, apart from their size, were poor architecturally and artistically.

The tombs of the end of the Old Kingdom and of the First Intermediate Period are generally of a simple plan and with minimum decoration. Many tombs in the cemetery of Pepy II at Saqqara bear witness to the already impoverished conditions at the latter part of his reign. Important officials of this period were buried in small mud-brick mastabas with a false door in the eastern façade. The burial chambers were shallow, small and roofed with mud-brick vaults (fig. 42). Their walls were frequently lined with stone and decorated with food offerings and an offering list. The tombs of lesser officials were even more modest. In provincial cemeteries of the period, e.g., those of Aswan, Thebes, Asyut and Dara, the majority of tombs consist merely of a small chapel, with a rather shallow shaft or a sloping passage leading to a small burial chamber. Generally the only decoration provided was a small stela placed at the mouth of the shaft or the passage. Even the apparently most powerful provincial governors of the time did not possess truly impressive tombs. Ankhtifi of Moalla, whose biography speaks of bringing Edfu under his control and of some kind of alliance with Aswan and part of Thebes, of his military strength, financial resources

Fig. 42 Mud-brick vault, Saqqara, late Old Kingdom

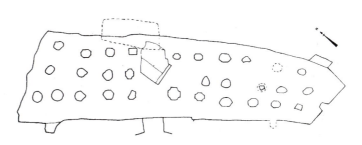

Fig. 43 Plan of the tomb of Ankhtifi, Moalla, Dynasty 8

Pl. 37 Unconventional art, Ankhtifi, Moalla, Dynasty 8

Pl. 38 Unconventional figures, Ankhtifi, Moalla, Dynasty 8

Pl. 39 Interior of a tomb at Beni Hasan, Dynasty 11

and of the important role he played in the power struggle in the southern section of Upper Egypt, presumably at the end of Dynasty 8, excavated one of the largest rock tombs of his time (fig. 43). Yet this is irregularly-shaped, with no walls at right angles, and with thirty pillars of different sizes and forms - some square, some round, and others of indefinite shape. Nor are these pillars symmetrically aligned, and all show cracks (for which the nature of the rock in the area is responsible) which are roughly repaired with plaster. The scenes depicted on the walls of the chapel are admittedly colourful, and perhaps show a departure from the usual Egyptian canon of art which is welcome to the modern viewer. But to the ancient Egyptian, such a style, where the figures are not perfectly proportioned, with thin long limbs, relatively small heads, large eyes and narrow shoulders and are 'floating' freely without the use of base lines, probably represented less able craftsmanship (pls. 37, 38). Such departures from traditional forms were caused by the lack of artistic influence from Memphis or from other major cultural centres in Upper Egypt. The tombs of Khety I and of other governors of the important province of Asyut, on the border between the kingdoms of Herakleopolis and Thebes when the country was divided into two factions, are also irregularly-shaped and demonstrate little architectural merit.

The Middle Kingdom

Egypt was reunified following the victory of the Thebans and the subsequent establishment of the so-called Middle Kingdom in the second half of the Eleventh Dynasty. The new kings firmly controlled the provincial governors who, unwillingly, one would imagine, had to relinquish most of the authority and independence which they had enjoyed during the First Intermediate Period. The most important tombs of Dynasty 11, therefore, are in Thebes and also in Beni Hasan, which perhaps supported Thebes in its struggles against Herakleopolis.

Chapels at Beni Hasan became less wide than deep, a feature which was rare in earlier periods, and were often approached through a small court. In their interior they generally had rows of pillars parallel to the entrance wall (pl. 39). The false door was still located in the west wall of the chapel or if a large niche was cut, in its west wall. At Thebes the tomb design was different. Greater emphasis was placed on a large court and an elaborate façade, which sometimes had a number of entrances leading to a narrow corridor parallel to the façade (figs. 44, 45). From this corridor, or from a single entrance in the façade, a long passage ran into the heart of the mountain, leading to a relatively small shrine (or cult place), then continuing, often in a descending slope, to a burial chamber. Both the shrine and the burial chamber were frequently cased with stone slabs and decorated. Only rarely was a serdab, blocked by a wall of masonry, created. Some of the corridors leading to the shrines were provided with steps, as in the tomb of Khety, and those which led to the burial chambers were sealed after the interment.

The Eleventh Dynasty did not last long, and the vizier of its last king established the Twelfth Dynasty under the name of Amenemhat I. He moved his capital to El-Lisht in the region of the Fayum, a more central position from which to govern the unified country, but perhaps also to escape the strongly loyal supporters of the ousted royal family of Dynasty 11.

Thebes, as a result, lost its special importance in Dynasty 12; one of the rare rich tombs found there from this period belonged to Antefoker and his wife Senet (fig. 46). The plan of the tomb was inspired by those of Dynasty 11. A court leads to the façade, in the centre of which is a doorway cased with stone and decorated in relief. This opens into a very long, narrow corridor, descending gently as it progresses into the heart of the mountain and leading to a square shrine. The door of the shrine is treated as an external door, as if the architect wanted to emphasise the secondary role of the long corridor as merely the means of access to the main shrine. The walls of the latter are plastered and decorated with painted scenes and inscriptions, while the ceiling is painted in red with black spots, probably in imitation of red granite. The plan thus far resembles the tombs of Dynasty 11, but the rest shows some originality. In the west wall of the shrine is cut a short corridor leading to a niche. While the corridor is decorated with scenes and a stela, a statue is placed in the niche which is walled off to create a serdab. Unlike the Eleventh Dynasty tombs, the long corridor does not continue beyond the shrine to lead to the burial chamber. The architect therefore followed the general design of Dynasty 11, but he introduced a shaft, separating the public area of the tomb from its substructure. These designs of the Theban tombs of Dynasties 11 and 12 were not followed in other centres, except perhaps to some extent at Aswan. They did, on the other hand, inspire the architects of the royal tombs of the New Kingdom.

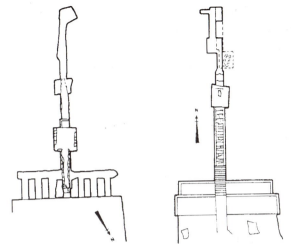

Fig. 44 (left) Plan of the tomb of Daga, Thebes, Dynasty 11
Fig. 45 (right) Plan of the tomb of Khety, Thebes, Dynasty 11

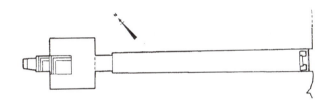

Fig. 46 Plan of the tomb of Antefoker, Thebes, Dynasty 12

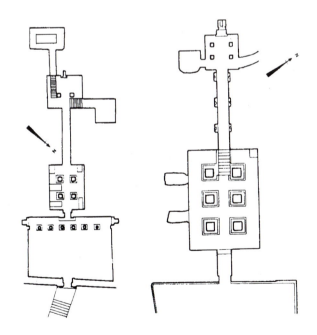

Fig. 47 (left) Plan of the tomb of Sarenput I, Aswan, Dynasty 12
Fig. 48 (right) Plan of the tomb of Sarenput II, Aswan, Dynasty 12

The Twelfth Dynasty tombs at Aswan are imposing (figs. 47, 48, pl. 34). As an example of these, one may cite the tomb of the governor Sarenput I from the reign of Senusert I. The tomb is cut at a height of 60 metres above the Nile River and is reached by a flight of stairs. A court and a six-pillared portico, constructed of white limestone and decorated in relief, lead to the façade of the tomb itself, which is cut into the rock. The doorway opens into a chapel, the roof of which is supported by two rows of two pillars each. From the chapel a long corridor leads to a shrine with two pillars and to a niche cut into the inner wall, axial to the long corridor and to the doorway. Two sloping passages open into the floor of the shrine and descend in steps towards burial chambers, one of which contains a burial pit excavated into the native rock. Like other tombs at Aswan, that of Sarenput I is very symmetrical, only the stairs leading up to the court are not axial to the doorway.

Another well known site that contains tombs dating to the Twelfth Dynasty is Beni Hasan. Although some of the tombs there are also impressive, they lack the grandeur and symmetry of the Aswan tombs. An example of the large tombs at Beni Hasan is that of Amenemhat. It consists of a court and a portico, the roof of which is carried on two pillars supporting an architrave. The façade of the tomb itself is cleanly cut into the rock of the mountain, with the doorway to the chapel opening in its centre. The jambs of the doorway are inscribed with Amenemhat's biography outlining the activities of his life. The chapel is a large room with four pillars set in two rows of two pillars each. A niche is cut into the inner (east) wall, axial to the entrance doorway, with a seated colossus and two smaller, standing statues of the owner sculpted in the native rock. The tomb has two rectangular shafts leading to the burial chambers (fig. 49).

Following the Twelfth Dynasty, Egypt entered an age of decadence which lead to the so-called Second Intermediate Period. Little is known of the tombs of this period, of which those at El-Kab and Hierakonpolis are the best preserved. On the whole, these are small, rectangular rock tombs with little evidence of lavishness or originality, although that of Ahmose, son of Ibana, at El-Kab has many attractive scenes and inscriptions.

TOMBS OF THE NEW KINGDOM AND THE RAMESSIDE PERIOD

The most important cemetery of the New Kingdom (Eighteenth and Nineteenth Dynasties) is that of Thebes, where tombs are distributed geographically over a number of sites. The important officials of the Eighteenth Dynasty cut their tombs into the higher slopes of Sheikh Abd-el-Qurna, while the lower slopes were left to less important officials. When one of these was promoted, he frequently cut

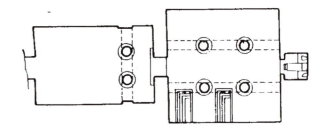

Fig. 49 Plan of the tomb of Amenemhat, Beni Hasan, Dynasty 12

a second tomb in the upper slopes, as did Menkheperrasoneb, owner of tomb No. 112, and later No. 86. More moderate officials were buried at Dra Abu-el-Naga. By the reign of Amenhotep III the higher level at Sheikh Abd-el-Qurna was crowded with tombs, and the important officials had to either locate their tombs in the lower level, e.g., tomb no. 55 of the vizier Ramose, or to move to new sites like El-Khokha and El-Asasif, which also had better quality stone.

The important Ramesside tombs were cut at Dra Abu-el-Naga south and in the lower level of Sheikh Abd-el-Qurna. Those found in the upper level of the latter site were sometimes usurped from earlier Eighteenth Dynasty tombs. The poorer tombs of the Ramesside Period were located at all sites, but mainly at Deir el-Medina. All of the above-mentioned sites continued in use until Dynasty 25, when they became over-crowded. The officials of the 25th and 26th Dynasties therefore constructed their tombs at El-Asasif.

Although they varied in details, the New Kingdom tombs shared the same general characteristics (fig. 50). The public area of the tomb consisted usually of a court, two halls and a shrine or cult room. The court was either totally cut into the face of the mountain, or was partly cut into the rock and partly constructed of mud-brick. Yet in many cases the court was simply a space left in front of the tomb. In the back wall of the court the doorway to the inner part of the tomb often had a large stela placed on either side, on which were represented the owner and his family at an offering table or in adoration before the gods. Within the tomb, the first hall was usually parallel to the façade. The second hall, perpendicular to the first and together with it forming a reversed T-shape, led to a small shrine with a niche cut into its back wall, axial to the main entrance. Certain tombs did not possess a separate shrine, in which case a niche was cut into the back wall of the second hall, still axial to the entrance doorway.

Rock-cut statues representing the tomb owner and members of his family were restricted to the niche during most of Dynasty 18. Starting from the reign of Amenhotep II, some of these statues were cut into the walls of one or other of the halls of the chapel. The statues, although restricted to the inner hall, became increasingly popular in the tombs at El-Amarna. This popularity of rock-cut statues lasted until the end of Dynasty 19, reaching a peak during the reign of Ramesses II when rock statues were used to decorate one or more parts of the tomb, including the façade, pillars or walls.

The ceiling of most of these tombs was flat, although instances of concave ceilings are known. In Dynasty 18, the ceilings were decorated with geometrical patterns, and towards the end of this dynasty birds and butterflies were introduced, probably influenced by the decoration of Amenhotep III's palace at Malkata (Western Thebes). The same designs continued in the tombs of the Ramesside Period, although religious scenes were also used.

If this was the general concept of tomb design in the New Kingdom, individual tombs certainly show variations. Some of these had pillars in the public area, or additional side rooms, or more than one niche in the shrine. Others, although less commonly, had one main hall instead of two. Certain tombs of the important officials from the reign of Queen Hatshepsut were influenced by the architecture of this queen's funerary temple. Rather than placing the outer and the inner parts of the public areas of the tomb at the same level, as were most tombs of the period, the court was divided into two levels connected by a ramp. Such is the case, for example, with the tomb of Senenmut (tomb No. 71).

The burial apartment, which could be formed of one or more chambers, was reached by a vertical shaft which opened into the floor of the chapel or of one of the halls of the tomb, or, more rarely, into the floor of the open court. More commonly, however, access to the burial apartment was by means of a

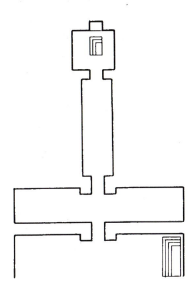

Fig. 50 The general design of the New Kingdom tombs at Thebes

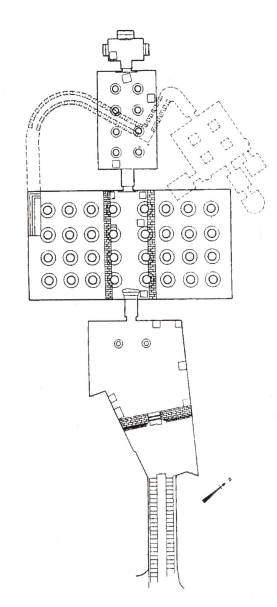

Fig. 51 Plan of the tomb of Ramose, Thebes, Dynasty 18

passage, either horizontal with its entrance cut into one of the walls, or sloping with its mouth cut into the floor in the public area of the tomb. These passages were usually short and straight during Dynasty 18 although some long and elaborate ones existed, e.g., those belonging to Senenmut at Deir el-Bahari from the reign of Queen Hatshepsut, and to the vizier Ramose from the reign of Amenhotep III/IV. Burial passages of the large tombs of the Ramesside Period were generally more elaborate, often spiral in shape, with a flight of steps.

The burial chambers were usually rough and undecorated, yet some were well-finished and nicely decorated. Those of Senenmut (tomb no. 71) and Amenemhat (tomb no. 82) have scenes of the

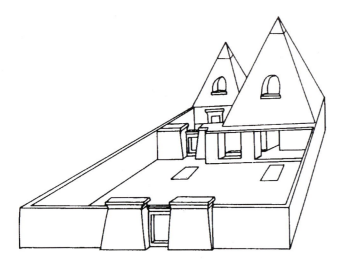

Fig 52 Reconstruction of a tomb at Deir el-Medina with constructed superstructure, New Kingdom

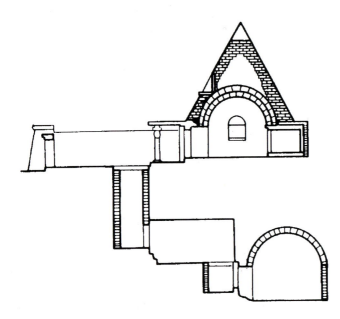

Fig. 53 Section of a constructed tomb at Deir el-Medina, New Kingdom

Netherworld. The roof of some burial chambers was often supported by pillars, as in the case of Ramose (tomb no. 55).

The tomb of Ramose, who served as vizier under Amenhotep III and his son Akhenaten, may be studied as an example of the important tombs of Dynasty 18 (fig. 51). The tomb follows the traditional plan of the New Kingdom tombs, but with the addition of pillars left in the rock to support the ceiling. A descent of 25 steps, with a continuous ramp in their centre (perhaps for lowering the sarcophagus), leads to an irregularly-shaped court. The doorway to the inner part of the tomb is cut into a plain façade. The ceiling of this hall is supported by 32 pillars in papyrus form. It should be mentioned that the design of this hall with its pillars is an exact copy in miniature of the great hypostyle hall of the temple of Luxor. The inner hall has 8 pillars arranged in two rows. An axial passage leads directly from the entrance of the tomb through the two halls and into the shrine. This is a small room without pillars but with three statue niches, the largest of which is in the back wall facing the entrance. The burial apartment is reached by a steep passage with steps on either side of a central ramp, not dissimilar to the arrangement of the descending approach to the open forecourt. The passage starts in the south-west corner of the outer hall and descends in almost a spiral shape to reach the burial chamber. This has four pillars supporting the ceiling and side chambers opening into its walls.

Tombs of Deir el-Medina

The tombs of Deir el-Medina, the necropolis of the artisans responsible for the cutting and decorating of the Theban tombs differ considerably from the usual design of the period, and should be described separately. Two types of tombs are known, constructed tombs and rock-cut tombs.

CONSTRUCTED TOMBS

The public areas of constructed tombs (fig. 52, 53) were built of mud-brick. A small pylon provided access to a walled court. It is possible that a basin of water was placed in this court and that some plants or even trees were grown. References to a kind of garden in the necropolis are found in texts from all periods. At the back end of the court a small pyramid was constructed of brick or stone, with the point at the top made of one piece of stone (usually called a pyramidion) which was decorated with scenes related to the solar cult. These pyramids were not influenced in shape by the well-known

Pl. 40
Burial apartment,
Sennedjem,
Thebes, Dynasty 19

ones of the Old Kingdom, but by those of the Middle Kingdom at Thebes. When the New Kingdom kings abandoned the building of pyramids in favour of rock tombs, the pyramid shape was adapted for use in some private tombs.

From the court, a doorway led into a rectangular chapel with a vaulted roof constructed within the masonry of the pyramid and decorated with funerary scenes in vivid colours. The chapel was often provided with a statue niche, as was sometimes the façade of the tomb. The substructure of the tomb was reached by a shaft or by rock-cut stairs which opened into the floor of the court. A corridor led to the burial apartment of one decorated room, or to a series of rooms of which the last was decorated (pl. 40). The walls of this vaulted room were usually cased with a layer of mud-brick, plastered, and decorated with painted scenes.

ROCK-CUT TOMBS

Rock-cut tombs (figs. 54, 55) were made in places where no flat area suitable for constructed tombs was available. The rock-cut façade of the tomb was provided with a portico carried on two pillars, and with rock-cut stelae and statues on either side of the entrance. The chapel consisted usually of two rooms: a large one often parallel to the façade, and a smaller one with a statue niche cut into its back wall.

Fig. 54 (top) Reconstruction of a rock-cut tomb at Deir el-Medina, New Kingdom

Fig. 55 (bottom) Section of a rock-cut tomb at Deir el-Medina, New Kingdom

The area above the entrance was flattened and a pyramid was constructed of brick or stone. The substructure differed from that of constructed tombs only in that access was gained from the second room of the chapel.

New Kingdom Tombs outside Thebes

The most important New Kingdom site outside Thebes is El-Amarna, the city constructed by Akhenaten of Dynasty 18. Although there is no consistency in their design, the private tombs at El-Amarna were certainly influenced by the general architectural features of the Theban rock tombs of the Eighteenth Dynasty. Basically, the public area of the tomb consisted of two halls, one perpendicular to the other. While at Thebes the two halls formed a

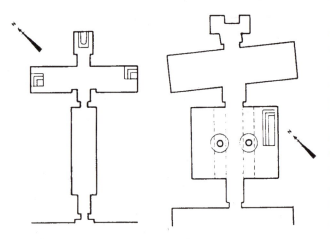

Fig. 56 (left) Plan of the tomb of Ahmose, El-Amarna, Dynasty 18
Fig. 57 (right) Plan of the tomb of Meryre II, El-Amarna, Dynasty 18

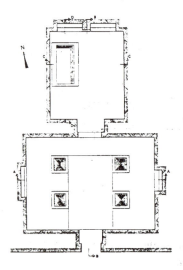

Fig. 58 Plan of the tomb of Onurismose, El-Mashayikh, Dynasty 19

reversed T-shape, with the doorway opening into the wide hall parallel to the façade, at El-Amarna the opposite was usually true, with the entrance leading into a long, narrow hall, although this is frequently no more than a short entry-way (figs. 56, 57). Like the Theban tombs, those at El-Amarna had a statue niche cut into the back wall of the inner hall, axial to the entrance. Yet here, in some instances, rock-cut statues also adorned other walls of the inner hall. Usually the burial chamber was reached by a vertical shaft situated at one end of the inner hall, but in some instances access was provided by a flight of stairs.

Variations to these general characteristics no doubt existed, yet it appears that the changes resulted merely from an individual desire to add pillars to one or both halls. The inclusion of pillars certainly increased the magnificence of the tomb, but caused little deviation from the usual design of the tomb.

Outside Thebes and El-Amarna, important tombs from the New Kingdom are rare. This was mainly the result of a return to a more centralised administration in this period, when the higher officials were buried in the capital. Of course, priests of local deities and some other administrative officials were still buried in the provinces, mostly in relatively modest tombs. Nevertheless, some of them left tombs of considerable beauty, as did Onurismose, a high priest of Re and Onuris in Thinis during the Nineteenth Dynasty, who cut his tomb at Naga el-Mashayikh to the north of Abydos. The tomb consists of two halls forming a reversed T-shape. The first hall, which is wider than deep, has four pillars arranged in two rows. The second hall, with a curved ceiling imitating a vault, is deeper and

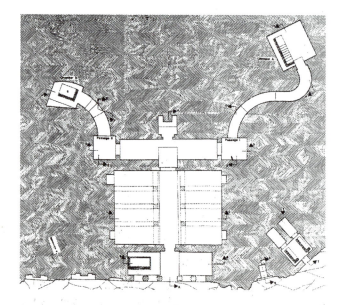

Fig. 59 Plan of the tomb of Sennedjem, Awlad Azzaz, Dynasty 18

has a niche in its back wall axial to the tomb entrance. A shaft, which opens from the inner hall, leads to a large and complex burial apartment (fig. 58). At Awlad Azzaz near Akhmim, the rock-cut tomb of Sennedjem, Overseer of Tutors, dated to the reign of Tutankhamun, is entered through an impressive high portico (fig. 59). The main pillared hall leads to a narrow broad hall and shrine. From both ends of this hall two winding passages lead to complex burial chambers. In many respects this tomb is not dissimilar to contemporary ones at Thebes.

Tombs in the other major centre of the time, Memphis, consisted of a superstructure constructed of stone or mud-brick and a substructure excavated into the rock. Some of these have lost a great deal of their stone through later quarrying, and others have not yet been systematically excavated and recorded. The tomb of General Horemheb, built at Saqqara before he attained the throne as the last king of Dynasty 18 and recently excavated and recorded, should serve as a reminder of the amount of information on architecture and on other aspects of Egyptian civilisation still buried under sand. Nevertheless, tombs of the New Kingdom and later periods differed to a greater extent from the earlier tomb designs based on domestic architecture. Increasingly the construction of tombs reflected the influence of temple architecture, and this was emphasised by the fact that the scenes now represented the owner involved in religious activities.

LATER DYNASTIES

The 25th and 26th Dynasties saw the last peak of tomb development, where large mud-brick pylons and large tombs were constructed at El-Asasif in Thebes, following the style of the Ramesside Period, but with huge subterranean complexes reflecting more the idea of the Netherworld. The main characteristic of the 26th Dynasty tomb, particularly at Saqqara and Abusir is its large rectangular pit which reaches 30 metres deep. At the bottom the burial chamber is constructed of limestone. This housed a limestone sarcophagus which in turn contained a wooden anthropoid coffin. The pit was filled with sand and the burial took place through a narrow subsidiary shaft connected to the burial

chamber by means of a passage. After the burial pottery jars which plugged holes in the roof of the chamber were broken letting the sand in the large pit fill the chamber. The necropolis workers left the chamber through the passage and from the subsidiary shaft. Anyone wanting to rob such a tomb had to empty the entire fill of the pit and the sand would keep streaming from the holes in the chamber's roof. While one of these tombs, that of Iufa, remained undisturbed until recently discovered at Abusir, most of its contemporaries were plundered in antiquity (fig. 60). This was not by emptying the main shaft, but by excavating a passage leading from the bottom of the subsidiary shaft under the burial chamber and then breaking into the sarcophagus from underneath.

Throughout their history the Egyptian never ceased to think and develop elaborate tomb designs to protect their body and the riches buried with it. But the wealth concealed in these tombs was too tempting for the less privileged classes and the ingenuity of the architects was certainly matched by that of the tomb robbers.

Fig. 60 Section in a 26th Dynasty tomb

III: TOMB SCENES AND INSCRIPTIONS

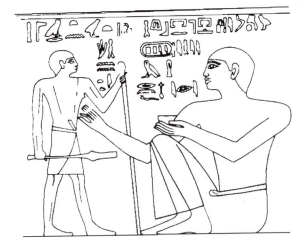

Fig. 61 Painting a statue, Pepyankh/Henikem, Meir, Dynasty 6

With the development of tombs from shallow graves to frequently elaborate mastabas and rock-cut tombs wall surfaces became available for use, in some periods and for certain individuals more than others, for the depiction of scenes and inscriptions. While these are usually referred to as tomb decoration, the term 'decoration' is used here with reluctance and for want of a better word which could describe the painting, relief and engaged statues occupying the walls of Egyptian tombs. To a large extent 'decoration' is a misleading term and should strictly speaking apply only to friezes which surround scenes and to some geometrical decorative motifs mainly on ceilings. Wall scenes themselves were almost certainly utilitarian. Whether they were intended to assist the deceased in their afterlife or to commemorate their life's achievements, their purpose was far from mere embellishment of the tomb.

ARTISTS AND CRAFTSMEN

There is a general tendency to consider the 'artist' who decorated the tombs as a 'craftsman', whose worth was based on his technical skills rather than on his individuality. While this view may apply to the majority of men in this profession, we should not stop searching for those mostly anonymous individuals who, despite the rigid rules and canons of Egyptian art, succeeded in leaving a personal touch here and there in their work and in some cases influenced the work of other contemporary and/or

succeeding artists. It is worth noting that art appears to have remained a male profession. The continuous need for men capable of satisfying the constant demand for artwork - decorated wall scenes, coffins, statues, etc. - meant that the profession could not rely only on the appearance of artistically gifted individuals. This, together with the conservative nature of the Egyptian, resulted in a type of art governed by very strict principles, and for the most part lacked spontaneity. These principles had to be taught carefully by the artist, usually to his son(s), rather than to people who demonstrated talent in the field. In such a tradition the likelihood of a genuine artist emerging was limited, but not impossible.

Representations of artists at work are usually restricted to sculptors and more rarely painters finishing off a statue or less commonly another funerary object. The depiction of sculptors or painters actually at work decorating the walls of a tomb is unattested. Because the bodies of statues, as with painted figures, were more or less stereotyped, it was possible for more than one sculptor to participate in the same job. Thus in the tomb of Ti at Saqqara for example, we see sculptors working in pairs on chiseling or polishing various parts of the bodies of statues. The same applies to the details of wigs which followed the fashion of the time, but does not seem to apply to the facial details which were presumably more personalised and required special artistic abilities, hence we see one sculptor polishing the face of a seated statue of Wepemnefert of Giza. Painters are also depicted colouring sculpted statues, as in the tombs of Meresankh III at Giza, Ankhmahor at Saqqara and Pepyankh/Henikem at Meir (fig. 61). The statues so represented are those of the tomb owner him/herself and sometimes other members of his or her immediate family; as, for example, in the tomb of Ankhmahor a group statue shows the tomb owner with his son. Infrequently, artists are shown handling other objects, such as in the tomb of Ibi at Deir el-Gebrawi, where a sculptor is cutting an image of a lion, while in the tomb of Pepyankh/Henikem at Meir painters are applying colours to a jar and a wooden chest.

Artists are often depicted at work in tomb wall scenes along with other craftsmen - carpenters, metal workers, leather workers, wine makers and jar manufacturers to name a few. Such a grouping does not automatically mean that they all shared the same workshop. Egyptian art has the tendency to group activities which are of similar nature, or which take place in similar environs. All the above-mentioned activities take place indoors, in workshops and ateliers, in contrast with other outdoor activities which are also gathered together in groups. Thus fishing, fowling, boatmen games and animals crossing the river are usually shown on the same wall or in close proximity to each other, while agricultural activities and animal husbandry are represented together and these are separate from desert animals and the hunt. Equally, the representation of the artist next to other craftsmen does not necessarily indicate that they all shared the same social status. Papyrus Lansing at the British Museum is a schoolbook written by a royal scribe to an apprentice, containing the advice to become a scribe and enumerating the difficulties and dangers of other professions, such as washermen, pot makers, carpenters, peasants, etc. Naturally, the advice is not totally objective and aims at giving the boy a dark picture of all occupations other than that of the scribe. However, the advice does not include the sculptors and painters, and in fact the latter must have been regarded almost as a special branch of the scribal profession, for the word painter in Egyptian is *sesh qedwet* which literally means 'scribe of the shapes/forms'. Indeed although initially written by scribes, the final version of tomb inscriptions, whether in relief or painting, had to be produced by an artist. Texts and scenes usually complemented each other on Egyptian walls, and probably this close relationship resulted in the Egyptian language maintaining its pictorial appearance.

Named Artists

While those responsible for the decoration of tombs remained in most cases anonymous, in a number of tombs the artists are named and are shown among members of the tomb owner's family and retainers. The sculptor Niankhptah is depicted in the tomb of Ptahhotep at Saqqara seated in a boat with a pile of food before him and a boy helping him to drink from a jar. The sculptor Neferihi appears twice with his master in the mastaba of Rashepses at Saqqara, and the sculptor Ptahkhewew is in the company of Werirni in the latter's tomb at Sheikh-Said. At El-Hawawish, the painter Khewenptah appears on a fowling trip in the company of the tomb owner, Kaihep, a governor of the province of Akhmim in Dynasty 6, and the same occurred again twice with the painter Seni, who is depicted in fishing trips accompanying two of Kaihep's descendants, a second Kaihep and Kheni. Such high regard for art

and artists at El-Hawawish may be explained by the fact that one of the forefathers of these governors was himself an artist; for in the tomb of the governor Nehwet, his eldest son and successor, Shepsipumin, stated that he was the painter who decorated his father's tomb. But appreciation of art was not restricted to El-Hawawish, for in the chapels of Mereruka and Khentika in the Teti cemetery the tomb owners are shown painting pictures of the seasons of the year. This does not indicate that these viziers were responsible for the decoration of their own tombs, but possibly represents the rendering of a temple calendar. At Meir and still from the Sixth Dynasty, the painter Iri is shown colouring an elaborate wooden chest in the presence of the tomb owner, Pepyankh/Henikem. In the tomb of Djau at Deir el-Gebrawi a long vertical inscription beside the staff of the tomb owner records the names and titles of the painter Pepyseneb/Nesi. As expected in areas where more tombs are decorated in relief than in painting more sculptors are commemorated, and vice versa. Thus named are the sculptors Djaam in the mastaba of Mereruka at Saqqara, Ptahshepses and Raireni in the mastaba of Ptahshepses at Abusir and Seni in the tomb of Ibi at Deir el-Gebrawi, among others. Occasionally a piece of work is attributed to a particular sculptor. An inscription records that the sculptor Itju was commissioned to carve the beautiful wooden door in the chapel of Kaemsenu at Saqqara, now in the Egyptian Museum, Cairo. From the New Kingdom the sculptor Iuty appears in the tomb of Huya at El-Amarna and from the Ramesside Period the painter Huwy is depicted in the tomb of Inherkhau at Deir el-Medina in Thebes with the surprising high rank of 'hereditary prince'.

Working Groups and Individual Artists

It is generally assumed that the decoration of large tombs was carried out by a group of sculptors and/or painters, probably under the supervision of a master artist. This view is corroborated by the fact that a close examination of the wall scenes in some tombs frequently reveals different levels of ability in various sections of the scenes. In the tomb of Ankhmahor, as in many large tombs in the Teti cemetery for example, the lower registers of most wall scenes are clearly better executed and contain more internal details. As these lower registers are more at the eye-level of the visitor to the tomb, it is likely that they were assigned to the more capable artists, who presumably were also older in age and were therefore allowed to work while standing on the ground or even seated on an elevated stool.

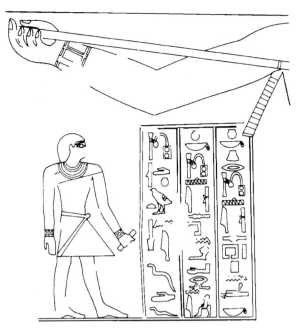

Fig. 62 Inscriptions of the artist Seni, Kaihep, El-Hawawish, Dynasty 6

Nevertheless, some tombs demonstrate an astonishing consistency of style and execution, which may be the result of the close and conscientious control by the main artist, or the fact that the whole decoration was the work of one man. The biographical inscriptions of the painter Seni, written in the Sixth Dynasty tombs of Kaihep and his son Kheni at El-Hawawish, show that the latter

Fig. 63 Tomb owner invoking, Inumin, Saqqara, Dynasty 6

alternative was sometimes the case. The inscriptions in the tomb of Kaihep read:

> The painter Seni says: It was I who decorated the tomb of count Kheni,
> and it was I also who decorated this tomb, I being alone (fig. 62).

There is nothing in the art of the two tombs that should make us doubt Seni's statement, nor does it seem likely that he would make an unfounded claim of this sort in a most conspicuous place in the tomb seen by the tomb owner, the contemporaries and the fellow painters, if these existed. Indeed the two tombs demonstrate great similarity in the subject matter, in the details and above all in the style and execution. In fact a study of the brush-strokes in both tombs show that these slant down from left to right and might suggest that our artist was left-handed. Seni was certainly a celebrity; not only was his work technically good, but it displays a great deal of originality. While Egyptian artists found great difficulties in dealing with foreshortening parts of the human body as a result of perspective, Seni's treatment of the hand holding the spear in a spear fishing scene and particularly the foreshortening of the fingers is both unusual and very successful (pl. 57). The consistency in style of the bold carving throughout the chapel of Ptahhotep at Saqqara might well suggest that here too, we are dealing with the work of one master sculptor, Niankhptah.

In judging the individuality of an Egyptian artist one should not be influenced by the repetitive repertoire of scenes, which was governed by their utilitarian purpose and the bounds imposed by the funerary beliefs. Instead, one should focus attention on the details in the main scenes, as well as on figures of workmen, animals, birds, etc, where the artist had more freedom to deviate from traditions and to experiment with the new. Therefore, while a cursory look at the same scenes in different tombs might give an impression of identicality, a careful examination of the details would give a completely different picture, for no two scenes are identical and it would be very wrong to think of the Egyptian artist as slavishly tied to the established conventions. Successful innovations frequently influenced other contemporaries, which makes it difficult in the majority of cases to attribute the decoration in more than one tomb to the same hand, or to be sure of the identity of the originator. However, with the continuous progress made in the dating techniques, it is now possible, in some cases, to place the examples of one theme in chronological order and to suggest its original source. In this respect the artist responsible for the decoration of the Sixth Dynasty mastaba of the vizier Kagemni in the Teti cemetery at Saqqara seems to have introduced new themes and developed some others. For the first time, as far as we know, the tomb owner was depicted on the façade of his tomb seated on a chair and extending one arm, palm up, in the so-called invoking posture, perhaps inviting the passer-by to present him with offerings or to recite an 'invocation-offering' formula for him. Such seated representations on the façade were copied by the decorators of the tombs of viziers in this cemetery (fig. 63), yet did not spread to other localities, with only one near contemporary example, that of Qar, known from Giza. While music and dancing are frequently shown in tombs, the artist of Kagemni's mastaba introduced in the theme a high kicking acrobatic movement by dancers which was imitated in

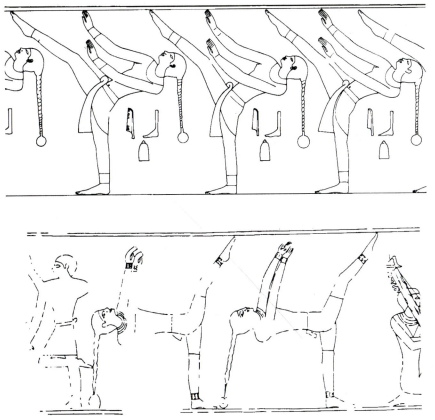

Fig. 64 (top) Dancers, Ankhmahor, Saqqara, Dynasty 6
Fig. 65 (bottom) Dancers, Kaihep, El-Hawawish, Dynasty 6

other tombs at Saqqara, but only in those of viziers. It is interesting however, to notice that Kagemni's artist was experimenting with a new posture, and therefore the dancers are shown with the leg on which they stand bent at the knee, resulting in an imbalanced posture where the weight of the whole body above the knee is thrown backwards without forward compensation. All other scenes at Saqqara and elsewhere have rectified the posture, creating a more successful balance by reducing or eliminating the bend at the knee of the leg on which the dancer stands and by keeping the torso more upright (figs. 64, 65). Nevertheless, Kagemni's artist gets the credit for introducing the movement in wall-scenes, and it appears that artists were particularly proud of their knowledge of depicting movements. The inscriptions on the Eleventh Dynasty stela of the sculptor Iritisen, now at the Louvre Museum, emphasise his ability to represent the body in different postures. He says:

> I can render the step forward of the male statue, the steps of the female statue, the movement of the wings of dozens of birds, the posture of someone smiting a captive and the expression of his counterpart. I can also render the fearful face of a

sacrificial victim and the posture of the arm of a hippopotamus hunter and the arrival of a runner.

Schools of Art

It seems likely that schools of art, perhaps influenced by the work of distinguished individuals, can be identified in particular localities at certain periods. The Teti cemetery at Saqqara almost certainly represents one of the important schools early in the Sixth Dynasty. Its work differs from the other important school at Giza, and each possibly exerted some influence on other provincial schools of art. It seems obvious that El-Hawawish for instance turned to Saqqara for inspiration, since the high kicking dance, for example, is attested only in these two sites. It is likely that the artist Seni of El-Hawawish was aware of the scenes at Saqqara, or was perhaps trained there.

Artists' Tombs

Tombs belonging to artists are few in number and do not display wealth, nor, in most cases, good quality art. While this may reflect the general financial means, and perhaps the relative social status of the artist, we should not forget that owning a tomb of any size in the official cemetery represented a privileged position. Among the tombs which belonged to artists are those of Rahotep and Ankhi at Saqqara and Sedaweg at Giza, but none of them demonstrates any richness in size or decoration or even in the level of craftsmanship. However, an inscription recorded in the Fourth Dynasty rock-tomb of Prince Nebemakhet at Giza indicates that a painter named Semerka and probably a sculptor called Inkaf made the tomb as a gift for the Prince. Whether they paid the labourers who cut the tomb, or only provided their own services free of charge, is uncertain, although the latter alternative seems more likely. Nevertheless, the artists must have been close enough to the Prince's family for such a gift to be accepted and publicly advertised, and equally must have had the means to support themselves during what must have been a relatively long project. Yet this was certainly not typical of the rather modest class of artist in ancient Egypt.

DECORATION TECHNIQUES

Relief and Painting

The type of decoration used was governed by the type of tomb and its building materials. In general, there seems to have been a preference for executing scenes and inscriptions in relief as opposed to painting. This was not restricted to any specific period or location. Reliefs were certainly more durable, and could at the same time be coloured, often with the addition of fine internal details. However, the decision between the two basic forms of decoration was hardly optional. In rock-cut tombs the quality of the native rock dictated the choice. In good, compact formation, relief was usually preferred. Examples of this may be seen in the Old Kingdom tombs cut in the cliffs at Meir, Deir el-Gebrawi and Aswan, and in some New Kingdom tombs at Thebes, particularly in the lower level of the cliff. In the majority of cases, though, the quality of rock, mostly formed of conglomerate limestone, did not allow a smooth surface on which relief could be cut, hence the use of plaster as a base for painted decoration. This is found, for instance, in the Old Kingdom tombs at Akhmim, some Middle Kingdom tombs at Meir and Beni Hasan, and many New Kingdom tombs at Thebes.

The plaster used varied according to the condition of the wall surface. If it was reasonably flat it was prepared for painting by being coated with a thin layer of gypsum/lime plaster, which could have been obtained by grinding the rubble from the cutting of the tomb in the limestone hills. On the other hand, if the quality of rock was poor and the surface obtained was uneven, a thick layer of plaster was needed. This was either of rough gypsum, mud mixed with straw, or brown clay found in certain cavities of some hills and also mixed with straw. Such thick plaster was then coated with a layer of a finer quality made purely of gypsum, or containing high proportions of it. In other instances, the rough plaster was simply covered with a thick wash of colour, in which case the straw may frequently be seen on the surface. Painting was most commonly executed upon plaster, yet cases exist of scenes painted directly on the smoothed rock surface, or of very shallow relief cut in the gypsum plaster.

The other type of tomb was the mastaba, which was either built of mud-brick or stone. In the case of mud-brick, the decoration was executed in painting on plaster. But frequently these mastabas had the walls of their chapels cased with slabs of limestone and, like other stone-built mastabas, were decorated with relief after the surface was polished and if required patched with plaster. Such is the type of tomb in the Memphite cemeteries of Giza and Saqqara at all periods, but particularly during the Old and New Kingdoms.

Reliefs were mainly of three types: a) incised, which means the outline and some details of the figures were engraved using a sharp-edged tool, b) sunken relief, where the outlines of figures were incised and the bodies were modelled so that their most raised parts are at the same level with the wall surface, c) raised relief, where the surface between the figures was cut deep, so that the modelled figures project outwards. In general incised and sunken reliefs produce more definite shadow lines when exposed to the sunlight; and because of this it was more suited for the external parts, like façades, of tombs, while raised relief was more common on the interior walls of chapels.

All scenes were first sketched in red paint and corrected in black, if necessary. The various colours were then applied, before a final outline was added, presumably by the master artist. Reliefs were frequently painted, which usually required covering them first with a very thin layer of plaster. The range of colours used by the Egyptian artist was limited: red-brown and yellow predominate. These are natural iron oxides and were mainly used to depict human bodies, some animals' skins, wooden objects, some food items, and so on. Blue and green were derived from copper frit and are often difficult to distinguish from each other. They were used to colour water, leaves, papyrus thickets, vegetables, etc. In addition, whitewash was used mainly for clothes and for the background, which could also be painted in grey, grey-blue, yellow or a creamish colour. Black, made of soot, was used to paint the hair and wigs, eyebrows and irises, yet this as well as the blue are two of the most impermanent colours and have disappeared from many scenes. These natural ingredients were ground and mixed with water and frequently gum, and were then applied to a dry surface, a process usually known as tempera. Fresco painting, in which the colour is mixed with lime and water and applied to wet plaster, was unknown in ancient Egypt. Despite his restricted palette, the Egyptian artist was able to produce different tones of one colour by diluting it with water. This was used to paint different objects in one scene. The artist was also capable of using the same technique to create shading, a more three-dimensional effect, as for example in the depiction of certain species of fish in the Old Kingdom tombs of Seankhuiptah at Saqqara (pl. 58) and Hesimin at Akhmim and the bodies of cattle in a census scene from the New Kingdom Theban tomb of Nebamun, now in the British Museum. But this technique was very rare and almost experimental, the most common use of each colour being as a flat tint. Another area where the artist showed his ability was by the application of white colour over body colour and frequently over pleated kilts, to indicate transparency or multiple layers of fabric.

Style

Egyptian wall scenes in tombs and elsewhere have peculiar characteristics which immediately distinguish them from the art produced by any other culture. In general, the Egyptian artist did not draw what he saw but what he knew. His picture, therefore, is not a true rendering of nature, but an intellectual composition in which he allowed himself to look at his subject from more than one angle at the same time, and to group together various subjects irrespective of locality and perspective. In three-dimensional art (statuary) the artist demonstrated his complete ability to depict the different parts of the body in correct proportion and perspective. By moving around a statue one could view every part of the body from its best angle. In two-dimensional art (painting and relief) the viewer obviously cannot do this, so the artist does it for him by depicting a subject from more than one angle at a time. Egyptian artists working in two-dimensions did not seem to have been worried, or perhaps even to have thought about perspective, depth, time and space in their compositions. Their aim was probably to draw each part of an object or a body from its most recognisable, and therefore most enduring

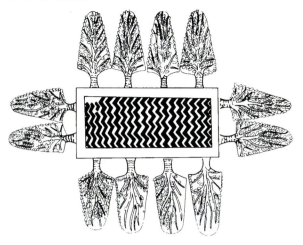

Fig. 66 Trees around a pool, Rekhmire, Thebes, Dynasty 18

angle. In drawing a garden for example the artist represented a rectangular pool in the centre, with fish on its surface rather than being submerged under water. Rows of trees surrounding the pool are then shown flat on the ground as this allows the most characteristic features of the trees to be seen (fig. 66). Since the viewer was familiar with such a technique, he had no difficulty understanding it. But, in order for us to appreciate fully such art, we must first be able to free ourselves from the judgement and taste conditioned in us by the principles of Greek and post-Greek art.

With regard to the human body, the Egyptian artist drew each part in its best and clearest aspect; thus the head is shown in profile with the eye and eyebrow fully frontal. The shoulders were represented in frontal view and the chest in profile with one nipple shown. The loin and hips were then twisted, revealing the navel and genitals, unless these were hidden under garments. Legs were drawn in profile and, except in rare instances where all toes are shown, are usually viewed from the inner side with both feet showing the big toe (fig. 67). Drawing hands seems to have caused even more difficulties. When the main figure faces right, usually the preferred direction, holding the staff in the left hand and the sceptre in the right, the hands are usually correctly drawn, as one can judge from the depiction or absence of fingers and nails. But in other situations the left and right hands are reversed. Presumably, to allow a left facing figure to hold the staff in the left hand without concealing part of the body, the artist placed the left hand on the right arm. Egyptian wall scenes are not, therefore, the depiction of what one sees in reality on a flat surface as is a photograph, but rather an interpretation of the different objects, or parts thereof, in order to convey the most unambiguous information to the viewer. To think that the Egyptian artist was incapable of accurately drawing the human body viewed from one angle would be a mistake; for the three-quarter back view of the serving girl in the New Kingdom tomb of Rekhmire at Thebes (fig. 68, pl. 41), or the frontal view of the female musicians, also from a New Kingdom mural scene now in the British Museum (pl. 59) , or the many depictions of statues being sculpted with their bodies perfectly shown in profile (fig. 69), testify to the artist's ability in treating this subject. Nevertheless, these remain exceptions to the rule, as the Egyptian artist generally drew a multiple-perspective picture of his subject, so that each detail would be represented from the angle at which it was best viewed and from which it was most easily recognised. With such a principle in mind, it is not strange to find that usually no other figure was allowed to hide any part of the tomb owner's body, and in fact every effort was made to avoid any part of his own body concealing another. Thus the individual, when standing, is normally stepping forward with the leg furthest from the viewer; when sitting the same leg is frequently moved forward, if only slightly, so that it is not totally concealed behind the other leg. In spear fishing scenes care was taken not to let the spear obscure part of the tomb owner's face. Similarly, the raised arm holding the throw-stick in fowling scenes never hides a face. In scenes of couples seated next to each other they are depicted as if one, usually the woman, is behind the other (fig. 70). In right facing figures, this can create problems not easily resolved, for in order to show the man on the woman's right, a traditional place, he was sometimes represented unrealistically hiding

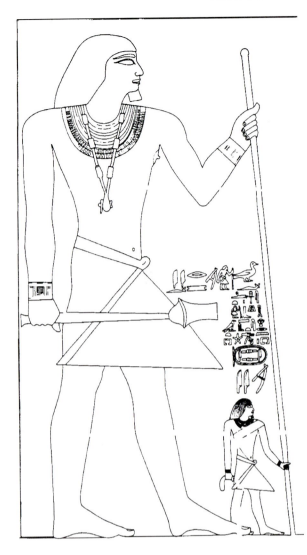

Fig. 67 Figure of the tomb owner, Nikauisesi, Saqqara, Dynasty 6

Fig. 68 Serving girls, Rekhmire, Thebes, Dynasty 18

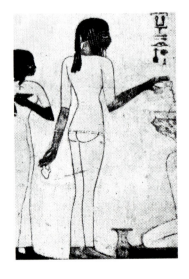

*Pl. 41
Detail of fig. 68,
Rekhmire, Thebes,
Dynasty 18*

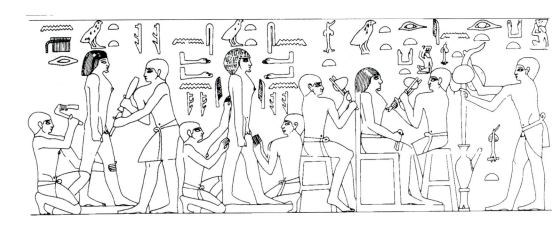

Fig. 69
Carving
statues, Ti,
Saqqara,
Dynasty 5

part of her body. The continuity of Egyptian art was broken only to a certain extent during the Amarna period under King Akhenaten. While the proportions of the body and its perfected style was not maintained, the rest of the cannon - such as the multiple perspective and comparative sizes etc. - remained.

Fig. 70 Seated husband and wife, stela, El-Hawawish, Dynasty 6

Size and Status

The tomb owner and some members of his family, commonly his wife and less frequently his eldest son, his parents or even a brother, are represented much larger in size than all other individuals in the tomb. This usually reflects his or her relative status. Yet it would be erroneous to use this same argument, as some do, to suggest that the wife has a lower social standing when she appears of much smaller size, crouching under her husband's seat or holding on to his leg (fig. 71). These seem to be symbolic representations of the wife, whose role

Fig. 71
(above)
Wife under
husband's
seat, Idu,
Giza,.
Dynasty 6

Fig. 72
(right)
Husband and
wife of equal
size,
Neferseshem-
ptah,
Saqqara,
Dynasty 6

79

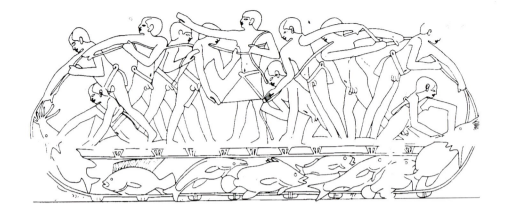

fig. 73
Fishermen at work,
Nikauisesi, Saqqara,
Dynasty 6

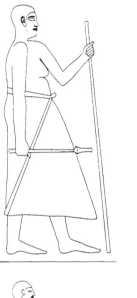

Fig. 74
Tomb owner at a
mature age,
Neferseshemre,
Saqqara, Dynasty 6

appears to be of secondary importance to the action depicted in the scene. The same wife, however, is often shown elsewhere in the tomb equal in size to her husband, regardless of the usual natural difference in height between men and women (fig. 72). The same criterion applies to men and women shown together, whether they belong to the upper classes as in the banquet scenes, or to the lower classes represented in the fields and workshops. While the tomb owner and his family are depicted in a dignified, almost stiffened attitude, the artist was much freer in representing minor figures, those of workmen, servants, etc., whose movements are more flexible, dynamic, varied and realistic (fig. 73).

Women also owned tombs in their own right, even outside the royal family. Nedjetempet, the mother of the vizier Mereruka had an independent tomb in the Teti cemetery. But husbands are never depicted in women's tombs and we may assume that this was because female tomb owners were unmarried, divorced, or that their husbands were long dead and that separate tombs were built for the women near their prominent sons in new cemeteries, as is probably the case of Nedjetempet. Otherwise women were usually buried in their husband's tomb.

Perfection and Affliction

Men were mostly, and women almost always, shown in a perfect, idealised form. While elderly men were represented with sagging breast and bulging stomach (fig. 74), representations of old women are very rare. More freedom was taken in depicting old age and even disabilities of workmen, who often appear too thin and weak (fig. 75), bald, suffering from hernia, etc. The last affliction appears both in the scrotum and navel and was rather common among fishermen and fowlers, two professions which obviously required sudden and concentrated effort in pulling the ropes of the nets (fig. 76). Faces were a different matter, and it seems that within the boundaries of the

Fig. 75 Emaciated herdsman, Senbi, Meir, Dynasty 12

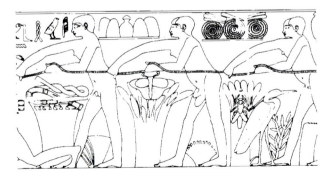

Fig. 76 A fowler with a hernia, Ankhmahor, Saqqara,
Dynasty 6

conventions laid down for him, the artist made a deliberate attempt to capture the predominant features of his subjects - such as the particular shape of the nose, lips, or chin - with varying degrees of success. The more we train our eyes to distinguish the subtle differences in their features, the more these people appear as individuals.

The Canon

Fig. 77 Artist's guidelines, Sneferuhotep, Giza, Dynasty 6

The main figures, and to a lesser extent the minor ones, were drawn according to an Egyptian canon, by which each part of the body occupied a certain proportion in relation to the whole. To achieve this, the wall was divided into grid lines to guide the artist. During the Old Kingdom only guidelines were used to mark the main points of the body (fig. 77). These were up to eight horizontal lines: the crown of the head, the hairline, the junction of the neck and shoulders, the armpits, the elbow, the lower border of the buttocks, the knee and the middle of the lower leg. Not all lines are regularly drawn in every scene, but most of them are found for example in the chapel of Nedjetempet in the Teti cemetery. Each figure was also marked by a vertical axial line passing by the ear and dividing the body into two parts. From the Middle Kingdom onwards the system of squared grids was used (fig. 78), with standing figures drawn on a grid of 18 squares and seated figures on 14 squares. The grid system varied slightly from one period to another. The grid lines are still visible in many scenes, particularly those left unfinished.

Conventions also determined the use of colours. A male body was painted in brick-red/brown while that of a female was yellow. If the picture included a series of men or women next to each other, they were given two different tones, the dark colour would usually alternate with the light in order to create a contrast.

Colour was also used to differentiate ethnic groups; thus Nubians appeared as very dark brown, Asiatics as light reddish. The dress was basically white, but sometimes had colour patterns, sometimes representing a bead-net worn over the dress. Frequently the clothes reveal the lines of the body underneath. Whether this was to represent the transparency of the fabric, or a mental image of what the artist knew existed, is uncertain but the latter seems more likely. Animals, birds, plants, food items etc. were painted in the closest colour to the original, and the same applies to the hieroglyphic signs. Thus, the signs representing a man or parts of the human body were painted in brick red, those depicting plants were green etc.

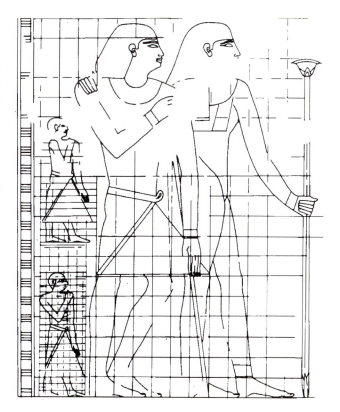

Fig. 78 Artist's grid lines, Senbi, Meir, Dynasty 12

Registers

Egyptian wall scenes are divided into horizontal registers, usually of almost similar height. The bottom of each register acted as a baseline for the figures depicted in it, without paying attention to spatial relationship. Thus, a number of overlapping men or beasts, for example would all have their feet/hooves on the same baseline. Subregisters were frequently used within the main registers. Their function varies, for they could be used to depict smaller figures, to create further wall space by dividing a register into two for the representations of minor figures, or to include in the main scene an individual or an object that logically should not be there. In scenes where all family members are shown, the inclusion for instance of a servant on a subregister allows him to be depicted without being considered as a member of the family. The scenes depicted in the registers of one wall are sometimes selected according to a logical grouping, for example, agricultural occupations, river activities, entertainment, or the like. Yet, elsewhere no coherence is apparent in the choice of the scenes, which are only linked together by a large figure of the tomb owner at one, or either end of the registers (fig. 79). If the different registers display successive steps of work - such as ploughing, sowing and reaping - the earliest of these was usually, but by no means regularly, placed in the upper register during the Old Kingdom, in the lower one during the New Kingdom, and in either during the Middle Kingdom. These arrangements may also indicate the relative distance from the viewer, something placed on a higher register may refer to a farther distance, yet no decline in the size or height of the different registers exists in either direction. This method of placing his subjects on different baselines denied the Egyptian artist the possibility of achieving a spatial

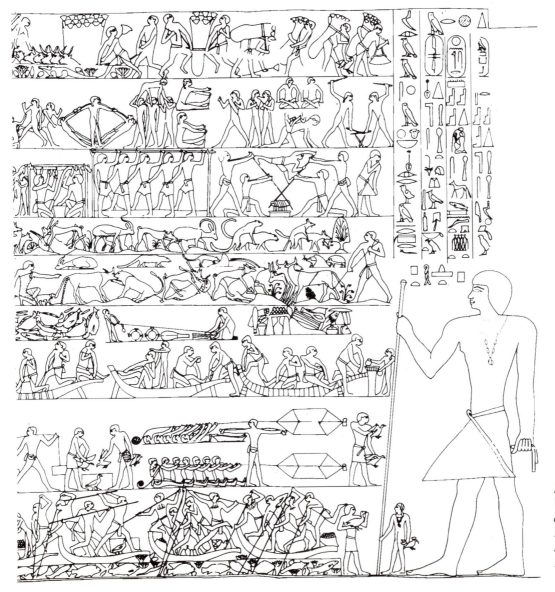

*Fig. 79
Watching various
activities,
Ptahhotep,
Saqqara,
Dynasty 6*

relationship or depth in his scenes. This was not through ignorance of such principles, but through a canon developed at the beginning of Egyptian history and accepted thereafter by the traditional Egyptian mind. It was more common for scenes from the Predynastic Period to be free from these baselines, and an example may be seen in the mural painting from Hierakonpolis. However, the Egyptian artist of the historic era did experiment with spatial relationships, as, for example, in the scene of brickmakers in the tomb of Rekhmire at Thebes (fig. 80), but particularly in crowded scenes showing fast movement, such as those of war and desert hunt (fig. 81), yet still avoiding the expected reduction in size of farther objects. But from the Egyptian point of view such scenes appeared rather chaotic. The artist was also successful in creating some perspective, for instance in the scene of the inspection of cattle from the Theban tomb of Nebamun, now in the British Museum, and in many other depictions of birds flying in different directions in the marshlands or in ceiling decoration. On the whole, the Egyptian artist was sensitive to nature and allowed himself more freedom in representing it. His paintings of the skins of various animals, the feathers of birds and the details of fish, were often superb and show great understanding and appreciation of the texture. Good examples of that

may be found in the Meydum geese, the fish and crocodile in the tomb of Seankhuiptah at Saqqara, and in the birds and animals in the tombs at Beni Hasan (pl. 60).

Another characteristic of Egyptian art is the combination of figures and inscriptions in the same scene, often leaving little empty space. Captions are added giving the names and titles of the tomb owner and members of his family, or indicating the activities he is watching or performing. Short phrases are also inscribed in front of the workmen, recording the dialogues that took place between them at work. These inscriptions form an integral part of a scene and are essential for its understanding. They also tell us a great deal about the various steps of any task and about the language, the humour and indeed the lot of the different classes and professions. Because the hieroglyphic script maintained its pictorial character, the inclusion of such texts in the scenes remains aesthetically appealing, even to the modern eye.

THEMES REPRESENTED

What influenced the choice of themes depicted in each tomb is uncertain, but it may well have been a combination of the owner's preferences and his

Fig. 80
Brick makers,
Rekhmire,
Thebes, Dynasty
18

Fig. 81
Desert hunt,
Senbi, Meir,
Dynasty 12

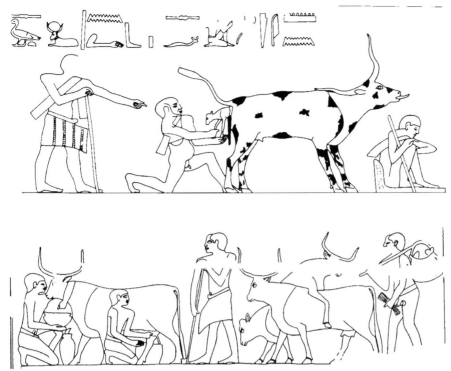

Fig. 82
Delivering a calf, Senbi,
Meir, Dynasty 12

Fig. 83
Milking, Nikauisesi,
Saqqara, Dynasty 6

profession, the artist's previous training, experience and taste, the customs of the period, the location of the tomb, and the amount of available wall surface. In the following discussion, themes will be differentiated as either 'regular' or 'incidental'. The former comprises scenes frequently found in well-decorated tombs and represent activities which could apply to any individual; the latter include a variety of memorable events which happened in the lives of certain men.

Because the regular themes - rural life, fishing, fowling, hunting, funerals, or even scenes of the Hereafter, such as the final judgement in the presence of Osiris or the work in the Field of Reeds - could apply to any person at any time, they are usually thought of as 'unspecific' or 'typical'. One wonders, however, if such scenes, despite their regular occurrence in tombs, did not represent moments which the tomb owner actually experienced, or depicted what he was expecting to

encounter in the Hereafter. The scenes were mainly added to the tomb for the benefit of the owner, not only to impress the visitors, and therefore, while lacking certain elements which render them as specific events to us, they were perhaps recognisable as such to him. The problem is that the Egyptian artist was bound by his repertoire and by the rigid rules which governed his methods of depiction, resulting in the close similarity of certain types of scenes. A careful examination of these scenes reveals some details which perhaps render them as more individual. In a scene where the owner watches rural activities, one may find a herdsman helping a cow giving birth to a calf (fig. 82), another milking a cow (fig. 83), bulls locked in combat, children fighting in a field being harvested, quail chicks picking some fallen grain, men catching the quails in a net (fig. 84), or the like. The fact that these events are also represented in other tombs should of course be expected, and should not

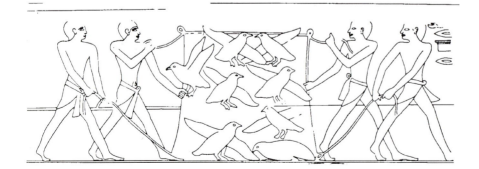

Fig. 84
Netting quails, Hesi,
Saqqara, Dynasty 6

automatically mean that the scenes are 'unspecific'. With similar surroundings throughout most of the country and considering the likely restraints imposed on the Egyptian artists, it is not surprising to find similar activities were set against similar backgrounds. However, the examination of minor details indicates that no two scenes are identical, and for the accustomed eyes of a contemporary Egyptian viewer these differences were perhaps sufficient to make the scenes specific.

Following is a brief survey of the scenes commonly represented in tombs, but many others may be found, particularly in the case of the 'incidental' scenes of which only a selection can be presented here.

REGULAR THEMES

THE TOMB OWNER AND HIS FAMILY

The commonest scene to be found in any tomb is that of the owner in front of food. As early as the Archaic Period, tomb stelae, the only decoration at the time, represent the tomb owner at an offering table laden with loaves of bread and other food items. This theme continues throughout Egyptian history with some variations in the number of loaves on the table, the type and height of the table, the shape of the chair on which the owner sits, the objects - ewers, basins, jars - placed under the table and the various food items stacked near the table. Frequently, the wife is shown next to, or opposite, her husband at the table, or crouched before a separate table (fig. 85). Offering bearers, including sometimes the children and other members of the tomb owner's family, are usually depicted carrying food and drink, live birds, flowers and leading small animals to him, and often to his wife. The different items carried and the variation in the movements of the men and the small animals usually make the scene more lively and avoid monotony (fig. 86). This theme was expanded much further in the New Kingdom to become an actual banquet attended by the family and acquaintances of the tomb owner, and included both food and entertainment. Thus in the

Fig. 85
Tomb owner and wife before food, Neferseshemptah, Saqqara, Dynasty 6

Fig. 86
Offering bearers, Ankhmahor, Saqqara, Dynasty 6

Pl. 42 A banquet, Nakht, Thebes, Dynasty 18

Pl. 43 At the tomb entrance, Nikauisesi, Saqqara, Dynasty 6

Eighteenth Dynasty tomb of Nakht at Thebes, we see the guests being entertained by musicians and dancers while eating and drinking (pl. 42).

Tomb owners are also frequently portrayed on the façades and entrances to their tombs. The commonest posture there is the one standing with a staff in one hand and the sceptre in the other (fig. 67, pl. 43). The majority of scenes show the tomb owner in the prime of life, but occasionally he is represented as a portly, mature-age man with pendulous breast, creases of fat across the body and bulgy stomach (fig. 74). Such figures are usually shown bare-headed, with an abbreviated shoulder and wearing a long, projecting kilt. On some façades, mainly in the Teti cemetery, tomb owners were depicted seated on a chair with one hand raised, palm up. The gesture may indicate an invitation to the passer-by to enter the tomb and perhaps present the deceased with offerings or simply invoke them (fig. 63, pl. 9).

Size as a Symbol

The owner of the tomb is usually portrayed as much larger in size than the rest of the figures, watching or participating in the activities displayed on the various walls of his chapel. His wife and children frequently accompany him in certain activities, in which case the wife is shown of equal size, that is, of equal status to her husband (fig. 72). But the same wife is sometimes symbolically represented as much smaller in size, under the chair of her seated husband or holding onto his leg (fig. 85). To think of such representations as reflecting her status would

certainly be wrong, for the same person could not be equal and at the same time so inferior. Egyptian art is full of symbolism, and it is possible that the inclusion of these small, illogical figures was meant to 'squeeze' into the scene an individual who was not or should not be there. In the spear fishing scene, for instance, it is almost impossible for the wife or children to be present in the small papyrus skiff (fig. 108), yet they are so depicted. If this interpretation was correct, then the Egyptian desire to symbolically be accompanied by his family has so far totally been misinterpreted. The children of the tomb owner were usually much smaller in size than

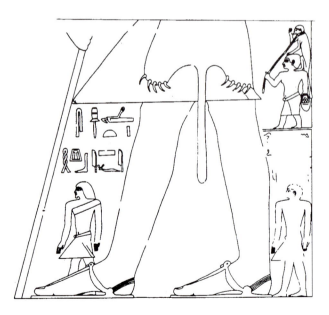

Fig. 87 Dwarf with a monkey, Ankhmahor, Saqqara, Dynasty 6

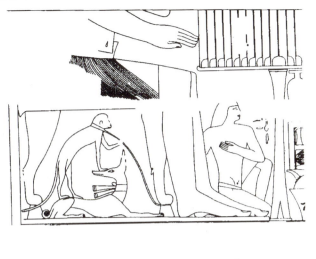

Pl. 44 (top left) Dwarf, pets and members of the family, Hesi, Saqqara, Dynasty 6

Fig. 88 (top right) Dog and monkey under seat, Inumin, Saqqara, Dynasty 6

Fig. 89 Wife playing the harp, Pepi, Meir, Dynasty 6

the parents, with the eldest child often shown bigger than the others, or even equal to his parents if he was already of age. Parents of tomb owners were not commonly represented in their children's tombs, which would normally be explained by their being deceased before the decoration of the tomb began. If they are present they appear of almost equal size with the tomb owner. It should be mentioned that in some of the best decorated tombs no wife and/or children appear. It is uncertain in such cases whether the tomb owner was divorced, a widower, unmarried or simply did not desire to represent his family in his tomb, although according to Egyptian traditions the last alternative seems unlikely. Servants and retainers frequently appear in tombs, sometimes with their names inscribed. Dwarfs also seem to have been favoured and were close to the family (fig. 87, pl. 44). Birds of many kinds are depicted, as are pet animals, the commonest of which are dogs and monkeys (fig. 88). These accompanied the tomb owner and dogs were often given names. The accurate depiction of details of numerous species of birds, fish and animals testifies to the artists' meticulous knowledge of nature. The tomb owner's house and garden were sometimes included in the repertoire of his tomb scenes, but this was not common.

Family Affection

In general and despite the 'formality' of Egyptian art, one cannot fail to see demonstrated love and tenderness between members of the family. Like Pepi of Meir (fig. 89), Mereruka and his wife are shown on a couch while she entertains him by playing the harp. He is also depicted holding hands with two of his sons in an affectionate manner. His closeness to his family was probably the reason for building a tomb for his mother Nedjetempet near his mastaba in the Teti cemetery at Saqqara, rather than burying her at Giza with his father, whom she presumably outlived. This same filial affection was the reason for Djau of Deir el-Gebrawi, at the end of Dynasty 6, building one tomb for both himself and his father, also named Djau, who died prematurely before building his own tomb. Djau left an inscription saying:

> I caused myself to be buried in one tomb with
>   this Djau in order that I
> might be with him in one place and not indeed
>   because there were not the
> means for building a second tomb. I did this in
>   order to see this Djau
> everyday, in order to be with him in one place.

RURAL LIFE

Given that ancient Egypt was basically a rural society, it is not surprising to find that scenes of agriculture and animal husbandry are most prominent in tomb decoration. Although many facets of agricultural pursuits are attested in tomb scenes, the commonest are those of ploughing and sowing, then harvesting. These are representations of the beginning and end of the process, with what occurred in between apparently being of less consequence. After the flood-water receded the sowing season began. Ploughmen worked in pairs using ploughs driven by cows or oxen to turn up the earth; one man drove the animals while the other pressed down the handles of the plough. Men with hoes usually accompanied the ploughing, either to mark the furrows or to break up the clods of earth. Other men, carrying bags of grain, scattered the seeds either in front of the plough so that they would be turned into the soil, or behind it, in which case a herd of rams was driven over the land to push the seeds into the ground. Although this is shown only in Old Kingdom tombs, Herodotus reported the use of pigs for the same purpose in the Fifth Century BC.

The Harvest

Harvesting was naturally the most important step in the agricultural process. Men were shown cutting the barley or wheat, usually high up the stalks, with the use of short sickles (fig. 90). Women and children collected the fallen grain. In the Old Kingdom donkeys were used to transport the bound sheaves to the threshing floor (fig. 91); in later periods labourers are depicted carrying the harvested crops hanging from poles. On the threshing floor the crop was spread in a circle and trodden by a herd of rams, donkeys or oxen. In the well decorated tomb of Mereruka the three species were successively used presumably to produce the best results. The animals were usually guided by men brandishing sticks to keep the animals moving and to prevent them filling their mouths with grain (fig. 92). The resulting grain and chaff were heaped and winnowed using long wooden forks and shallow scoops, the latter being employed mostly by women and children who fling the mixture in the air, allowing the chaff to fly away and the grain to fall (fig. 93). Finally, women use sieves to remove the last impurities from the grain. However, the level of wear in Egyptian teeth suggests that sieving was not very successful. After this the grain was measured, recorded by the scribes and stored in granaries (fig. 94). Close to the scenes of harvesting the barley or wheat men are usually shown pulling flax for making linen.

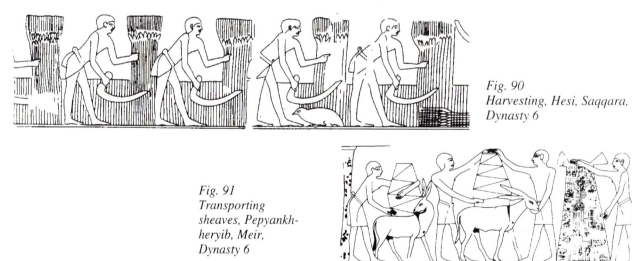

Fig. 90
Harvesting, Hesi, Saqqara,
Dynasty 6

Fig. 91
Transporting
sheaves, Pepyankh-
heryib, Meir,
Dynasty 6

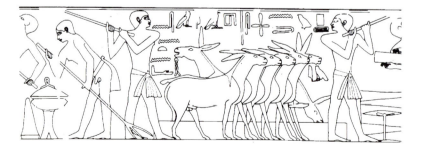

Fig. 92
The threshing floor, Ankhmahor, Saqqara,
Dynasty 6

Fig. 93
Winnowing, Ankhmahor, Saqqara, Dynasty 6

Fig. 94
Measuring the grain, Nikauisesi, Saqqara, Dynasty 6

The Peasants

Since the harvest season was in summer, the field workers periodically needed drinks; beer was the common beverage. The scenes and their accompanying captions generally reflect a happy atmosphere, often with a flute player present (fig. 95). One need not take literally the words of some ancient Egyptian writers who described the hard life of the peasants and other manual labourers. Such literature aimed at encouraging the young students and future scribes to study hard by indicating to them the difficulties of other occupations, and accordingly, could hardly have been totally objective. Nevertheless, scenes which depict farmers or herdsmen being beaten in the presence of scribes exist, particularly from the Old Kingdom (fig. 96). The accused were led by men holding sticks to be questioned by the scribes. Culpable men were then forced to prostrate themselves and were beaten. In the tombs of Mereruka and Khentika in the Teti cemetery the guilty peasants were held naked against a wooden pole and beaten. It is possible that such punishment was necessary in some instances to extract missing amounts of produce or the correct amount of taxes from dishonest farmers. However, the frequency of such scenes is so small that we cannot assume that dishonesty was a widespread problem. In the New Kingdom the officials measured the crop with a tape and assessed the taxes before the harvest, which appears to have succeeded in removing the need for frequent punishment.

Fruit and Vegetables

Plantations of various fruits and vegetables are less often represented, although the produce of these is regularly shown on the offering tables. Moreover, a few scenes have survived of fruit picking, mainly figs and grapes. Men are shown near and on trees collecting the figs in trays, or under a vine gathering clusters of grapes in containers (fig. 97). The latter activity is usually associated with wall scenes of wine making (pl. 62). In New Kingdom tombs gardens with fruit trees are painted (fig. 98, pl. 61); popular among these were grapevines, figs and dates. Such gardens were sometimes watered using the shaduf (fig. 99), a lifting device still used in Egypt today.

Fig. 95 Flute player in the field, Ti, Saqqara, Dynasty 5

Fig. 96 Punishment scene, Ti, Saqqara, Dynasty 5

Fig. 97
Picking grapes, Shedu, Deshasha,
Dynasty 6

Care for Animals

Animal breeding features prominently in tomb scenes and demonstrates the Egyptians' knowledge of, and care for, their animals and the artists' familiarity with the subject. Herdsmen are shown leading their animals, tending them if sick, force-feeding them, milking cows, etc. Scenes of mating and of cows giving birth, often helped by a herdsman, are also frequent (figs. 82, 83). Animal reproduction was certainly foremost in the mind of the Egyptian, and that was not restricted to agriculture and domestic animals, but was extended to nature in general, including wild birds and animals as well as aquatic animals. Depictions of bulls fighting are not uncommon, but are restricted to Upper Egyptian tombs. The significance of such representations is disputed. Some think the fights were accidental and aimed at winning a cow. Others believe that these were not chance conflicts but organised events with the view of selecting the strongest bull for breeding purposes. Some also think that they were displays for the amusement of spectators. The last view agrees with the account of Strabo, who wrote at the end of the First Century BC and the beginning of the First Century AD that 'it is the custom to organise contest between bulls which are bred by certain individuals for that specific purpose, after the fashion of horse-breeding, for they let them loose and get them to fight and the one considered the stronger wins a prize'. Examples of bull fighting scenes are found in most of the Upper Egyptian sites, but particularly at El-Hawawish, El-Hagarsa, Meir, El-Bersha and Deshasha (figs. 100, 101). Characteristic of the Old Kingdom are scenes of cattle crossing a river preceded by the herdsmen in a papyrus boat or by one of them carrying a calf on his shoulders to entice the mother and the herd to follow. This was always a dangerous time for the water contained aquatic animals, particularly crocodiles, which were ready to attack the herd.

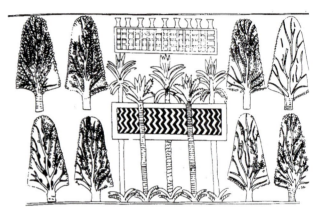

Fig. 98 Garden with fruit trees, Rekhmire, Thebes, Dynasty 18

Fig. 99 Shaduf, Ipy, Thebes, Dynasty 19

These scenes, as the one in the tomb of Ankhmahor, show the herdsmen uttering special spells to drive the crocodiles away, or to blind them to the herd (fig. 102).

As well as cows and oxen, there are also represented donkeys, sheep, goats, and even pigs, although there are few examples of the last. The picture of goats standing up against a small tree in order to browse is seen in many tombs. The

Fig. 100
Bulls fighting, Mery, El-Hagarsa, Dynasty 6

Fig. 101
Bulls in combat, Ukh-hotep, Meir, Dynasty 12

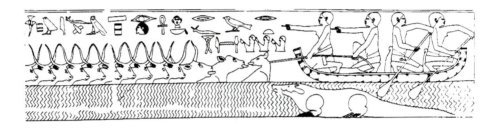

Fig. 102
Cattle crossing the river, Ankhmahor, Saqqara, Dynasty 6

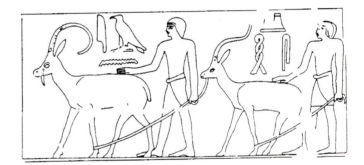

Fig. 103
Ibex and gazelle, Seankhuiptah, Saqqara, Dynasty 6

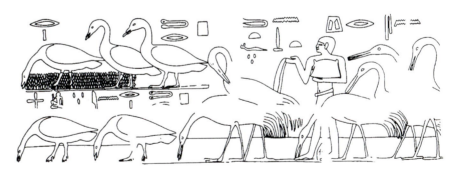

Fig. 104
Geese and Cranes, Nikauisesi, Saqqara, Dynasty 6

Egyptian seems also to have domesticated some wild animals, such as gazelles, oryxes and hyenas, but again these seem to be more common during the Old Kingdom (fig. 103). Of the domestic fowl, a variety of species of ducks, geese and even cranes are represented (fig. 104). These animals and birds formed an essential part of the Egyptian diet and are regularly present in offering scenes. Pet animals were frequently depicted in close proximity to the tomb owners. Dogs and monkeys were the favourites (fig. 88), but cats and more rarely leopards or lions, for royalty, were also domesticated.

Fig. 105 Fishing with a large net, Hesi, Saqqara, Dynasty 6

FISHING, FOWLING AND DESERT HUNTING

Fig. 106 Fishing with a hand net and line, Idut, Saqqara, Dynasty 6

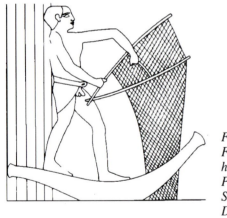

Fig. 107 Fishing with a hand net, Ptahhotep, Saqqara, Dynasty 6

Pl. 45 Fishing with basket traps, Hesi, Saqqara, Dynasty 6

In a country which literally lived on the banks of a river rich in aquatic life, with extended marshlands in the north where wild birds nested, and bordered on both east and west by deserts which, at least in its early history, appear to have been densely inhabited by wild animals, it is only natural to find that fishing, fowling and hunting were practised widely by the Egyptian, and were commonly represented in his tomb, both as professions and sports.

Fishing

Fishing as a profession involved the use of large nets operated by a team of fishermen from the shore or from boats, or by means of small hand nets, weirs, basket traps or lines with hooks held by the individuals (figs. 105-107, pl. 45). The tomb of Hesi in the Teti cemetery depicts most of these fishing techniques. Artists took the liberty in such scenes to show a variety of movements in the postures of the men involved. They also depicted some of them suffering certain afflictions, such as scrotal and navel hernias, typical of professions that require sudden, strong effort. Artists also demonstrate great knowledge of the various species of fish and of the different fishing techniques, but unfortunately, not of the species most likely to be caught by each method. Thus hand nets are usually used in shallow water, yet they are shown catching Lates, generally a deep, open water species.

With fish being abundant, as one may gather from tomb scenes, some of the catch had to be cut open, cleaned, laid flat or hung to dry and be preserved. Market scenes show the selling and buying of both fresh and processed fish, as seen for instance in the tomb of Ankhmahor at Saqqara (fig. 128).

Fig. 108
Spear fishing,
Pepyankh/
Henikem, Meir,
Dynasty 6

Considering the popularity of fishing scenes in tombs it is astonishing that fish are never shown as being presented for consumption to the tomb owner, or even included in the inscribed lists of offerings which he desired. Surely fish formed an important part of the Egyptian diet since the tomb owner himself is portrayed supervising its production, but whether it was consumed by all classes or only by the lower ones is debatable. The absence of fish from among offerings may not at all be related to taste, or class distinction but to the fact that it was probably considered unclean and inappropriate for the purity of the tomb. In the hieroglyphic language a fish is used as the determinative for words like 'abomination', 'detested' and 'stink'. In fact in Spell 64 of the Book of the Dead it is clearly stated that

'one shall recite this spell only when he is pure and spotless, without eating goats or fish or going near women'. It is interesting that as early as the beginning of the Sixth Dynasty the vizier Hesi expressed the same concept by inscribing on the entrance to his tomb in the Teti cemetery a request for visitors not to enter the tomb if they have eaten abominations (with the fish determinative) or have copulated with women.

As a sport fishing was only practised by the tomb owner and his family, who are always shown successfully spearing two large fish, a Lates and a Tilapia (fig. 108). It is curious that these two species prefer completely different habitats and the chance of spearing them together is minimal. Whether the Egyptians were aware of such a difficulty, and

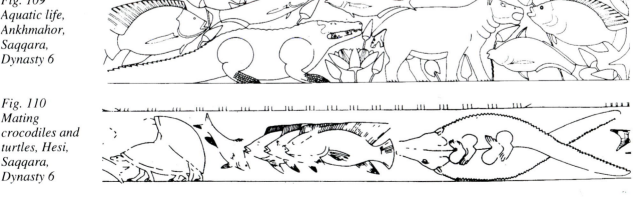

Fig. 109
Aquatic life,
Ankhmahor,
Saqqara,
Dynasty 6

Fig. 110
Mating
crocodiles and
turtles, Hesi,
Saqqara,
Dynasty 6

Fig. 111 Hippopotamus hunt, Idut, Saqqara, Dynasty 6

to the level of his spear. The angle at which the spear was held varied from nearly horizontal to approximately 20 degrees during the Old Kingdom. During the New Kingdom the 'mound of water' was much shorter which resulted in the spear depicted at a much steeper angle. In addition to the two large fish the 'mound of water' included some other species, and usually rich aquatic life was shown in the water beneath the tomb owner's papyrus boat. Of the familiar motifs are the fight between a hippopotamus and a crocodile, the former invariably being the winner, and a crocodile waiting to snatch a newborn hippopotamus (fig. 109). The very rare motifs include a crocodile laying eggs and two mating crocodiles or turtles (fig. 110). Animal behaviour in such an environ was difficult to observe, hence its rarity. However, such scenes appear in the tombs of Mehu, Kagemni and Hesi at Saqqara.

therefore catching these two fish, in particular, became an achievement worthy of recording, or whether they were simply attaching to the spear two fish they prefer remains uncertain. Some also regard the two types of fish as representing two parts of the country and others see a connection between the Tilapia and reproduction. But before accepting one interpretation or the other, we have to bear in mind the consistency in depicting the two species throughout Egyptian history and the fact that spear fishing is by no means a commonly depicted theme in all, or most tombs. Nikauisesi of the Teti cemetery, for instance, represented himself fowling with a throw-stick, but not spear fishing.

Fishing with a line and multiple hooks was also common and appears to be always successful. In the Old Kingdom this was practised by fishermen in small papyrus boats, but in later periods this became a method of entertainment for the tomb owner who is occasionally depicted seated on a chair fishing with a line from ashore.

To maintain a dignified posture while spearing fish the tomb owner in the Old Kingdom was not shown bending down, but rather the water was represented like a 'mound' which brought the fish

Close to spear fishing scenes is the frequently depicted activity of a hippopotamus hunt. Being dangerous, this was not undertaken by the tomb owner, but by some of his followers. The episode most familiar is that of a few men holding the harpoon in one hand and in the other the ropes attached to the barbs which have been embedded in the victim's body. As expected, the animal is shown agitated and in great pain (fig. 111).

Fig. 112 Fowlers and clap-nets, Ankhmahor, Saqqara, Dynasty 6

Fig. 113
Fowling with a
throw- stick,
Pepyankh/
Henikem, Meir,
Dynasty 6

Fowling

The marshlands of the Delta were not only rich in fish and aquatic animals, but were also the natural habitat for a wide variety of birds. Professional fowlers used clap-nets to catch these birds. The nets were set amidst aquatic vegetation and the environment was rendered realistically by the presence of various insects, grasshoppers,

Pl. 46 The marshland, Hesi, Saqqara, Dynasty 6

dragonflies, etc. Water weeds and frogs were also shown. With a good grip on the rope attached to the net, the haulers stood ready, supervised by an overseer. When enough birds have gathered on the net then comes the most important moment of the hunt. The overseer gives the signal, the men pull the rope, throwing themselves backwards to the ground to close the net firmly. The following moments are full of action; with men collecting the birds from the net and putting them in cages (fig. 112).

Fowling with a throw-stick was a sport enjoyed by some tomb owners. This, like the spear fishing, was practised in the marshland which is represented as a thick papyrus bush rich in birds flying, standing on a papyrus umbel or nesting. Commonly depicted are genets and Egyptian mongooses climbing the stalks, which bend under their weight, to snatch the fledglings. The parent birds usually defend the young ones by attacking the predators, but in most cases unsuccessfully (pl. 46). Using a papyrus skiff, the tomb owner passes through the thicket, with some decoy birds in one hand and the throw-stick in the other (fig. 113). In Old Kingdom scenes no bird is shown being hit, as is the case in the New Kingdom. As the Egyptian throw-stick was different from the boomerang in that it did not return to the thrower, numerous sticks were needed, and family members and retainers carrying them are usually shown accompanying the tomb owner. In the proximity of fowling scenes the preparation of the catch for consumption is often shown. Men are plucking birds or crouching and roasting some on an open fire.

Many other activities took place in the marshland; repairing boats, or making new ones out of papyrus, or sometimes wood. Men are shown uprooting papyrus stems, tying them in bundles which they carry on their backs, and binding them tightly with rounds of ropes to form the boats. Carpenters are sometimes represented with adzes and saws constructing wooden boats.

Water Games

As with other professions, the work atmosphere seems to have been both energetic and pleasurable. Boatmen frequently staged a mock fight which appears to be a lively game which tomb owners

enjoyed watching. Two groups of boatmen in skiffs try to push each other into the water using long poles. Men were sometimes carried away by their enthusiasm, overlooking the presence of crocodiles and subjecting their comrades to real danger by pushing them into the water. Sometimes the game seems also to exceed acceptable pleasantry. Members of one team are for instance shown about to deliver to their counterparts blows to the head using clubs or throw-sticks. In the tomb of Inumin in the Teti cemetery men in the prows of the two opposing boats are grasping each other by the genitals, while being watched by the tomb owner, who leans on his staff in a relaxed posture, accompanied by his wife (fig. 114).

Hunting

Unlike in present day, the Egyptian cliffs and deserts

Fig. 114
Mock fight between boatmen, Inumin, Saqqara, Dynasty 6

Fig. 115 *Hunting dogs attacking an oryx, Inumin, Saqqara, Dynasty 6*

Fig. 116 *Force-feeding hyenas, Inumin, Saqqara, Dynasty 6*

had more rainfall and were richly inhabited by wild animals, which from the beginning provided many of the necessities of life for the dwellers of the Nile valley. Common among these animals were gazelles, ibexes, oryxes, hyenas, jackals, foxes and wild asses, but also depicted were lions, leopards, hares, hedgehogs and jerboas. During the Old Kingdom hunting was on foot, while in the New Kingdom chariots were also used. However, hunting scenes become rare after the reign of Thutmose III. In the earlier period the lasso and the hunting dogs were used, but from the end of the Old Kingdom onwards shooting with bows and arrows became common. Hunting did not only take place in deserts, but kings and rich tomb owners practiced this sport in large enclosures after the animals were driven into them by servants. The hunter could in this case enjoy the thrill of the hunt and the safety of shooting from outside the fence of the enclosure. Scenes show hounds attacking the injured animals and in the tombs of Mereruka and Inumin in the Teti cemetery, this theme was expanded to show an oryx being pulled apart by nine and ten dogs respectively, with the tomb owner watching, but not participating in the activity (fig. 115).

Egyptians were apparently also successful in taming many of the wild animals they captured alive, and we see some of these led by offering bearers to be presented to the tomb owner. Scenes, particularly from the Old Kingdom, as that in the tomb of Inumin at Saqqara, show the force-feeding of hyenas and other wild animals, presumably to fatten them for the table (fig. 116). In all these scenes the artist showed particular understanding and sensitivity to animals, both domesticated and wild, with correct detailing of their shapes and movements.

PROFESSIONS AND INDUSTRIES

Carpentry

Numerous activities of various professions are represented in tomb scenes. Common is a carpenter sawing a plank of wood or using his adze or chisel to shape objects (fig. 117, pl. 47). The finished products often appear close by: beds, chairs, head-rests, chests, draught-boards, scribal palettes, etc. With local woods being both limited and of an ordinary quality, carpenters developed special abilities in building large wooden surfaces out of small planks, using tenons and mortises, or wooden pegs to join them. These planks were used in the construction of large objects such as coffins and ship hulls, the former being one of the most demanded objects, while the latter perhaps required the greatest skills. Many objects were made of imported wood; the good cedar timber from Phoenicia was essential for ship masts and was particularly valued, as was the ebony from Africa and other rare woods which were painted in scenes in colours sufficiently accurate to enable their identification. Imported woods were presumably destined for the royal workshops to produce objects for various temples, royalty and the top administrators. Staffs were needed and their manufacture is vividly recorded, with a group of men using the pressure of their weight and muscles to straighten and adjust tree branches (fig. 118).

Metal Work

Metal workers are frequently depicted beside carpenters. A common representation in the Old Kingdom is that of men blowing air into the fire through long pipes to smelt the metal, mainly copper from Sinai. These pipes allow the workers to keep their distance from the intense heat, against which

they sometimes protect their faces with one hand (fig. 119). In the New Kingdom, as in the tomb of Rekhmire at Thebes, the air was fed to the fire from bellows operated by men, each man using two bags, throwing his weight from one bag to the other. Men are also shown pouring the molten metal, or beating it into shape. The different steps of metal work are better represented in the New Kingdom tombs,

Fig. 117 Carpenters at work, Shedu, Deshasha, Dynasty 6

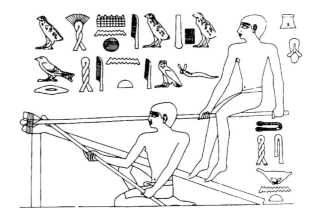

Fig. 118 Making staffs, Ti, Saqqara, Dynasty 5

Pl. 47 Carpenters at work, Ti, Saqqara, Dynasty 5

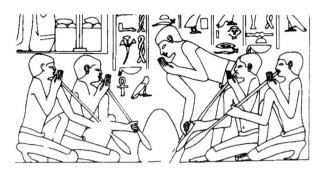

Fig. 119 Metal workers, Ankhmahor, Saqqara, Dynasty 6

where one also sees the weighing, polishing, incising, etc. processes. Jewellers were included among the metal workers, although they held a higher status. In the Old Kingdom this profession was often undertaken by dwarfs (fig. 120). Scenes

Wine Making

Many industries were based on agricultural produce. Wine making, for instance, is depicted in a number of tombs from the Old Kingdom onwards, and it was most probably known in the Prehistoric era. Wine, which was considered a luxury drink by comparison with beer, was made from grapes, dates, figs or other fruits. Grapes were first trodden by men in large vats, from which the juice was collected through a spout (pl. 62). The sediment was then put in a cloth sack and squeezed to extract the remaining must. This was achieved by twisting poles attached to the two ends of the sack by men performing almost acrobatic actions (fig. 121). A baboon is often added as if participating in the work, providing a lighthearted touch to the scene. The juice was then filtered into a large fermentation container before it

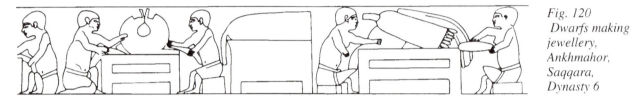

Fig. 120 Dwarfs making jewellery, Ankhmahor, Saqqara, Dynasty 6

was transferred into wine jars for consumption or storage, the latter were sealed with clay stoppers, impressed with the type and vintage.

Brewing and Bread Making

Bread and beer represented the staple diet of the ancient Egyptian and are accordingly shown frequently in tomb scenes. The two items share to a large extent the same ingredients and some steps of manufacturing and for this they are usually associated in the scenes (fig. 122). The most common grains in Egypt were emmer wheat and barley, from which flour was made first by pounding, using stone mortars and pestles, then by grinding using grinding stones. With such tools it was inevitable for grit to find its way into the flour and bread, resulting in advanced tooth wear among Egyptians at a relatively young age. The flour was partly cleaned using sieves made from rushes, then kneaded into dough. Various types of breads are known, but the commonest are the flat, round loaf and that shaped and baked in pottery moulds.

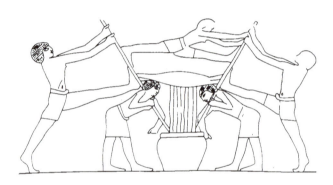

Fig. 121 Wine pressing, Mereruka, Dynasty 6

as that in the tomb of Ankhmahor, depict the weighing of gold ingots using a balance, melting the metal using a furnace, beating the metal into shape using rounded stones and finally producing gold objects such as pendants, earrings, collars, etc. Jewellery was adorned by the addition of semi-precious stones, such as turquoise, lapis-lazuli and carnelian. Gold was also beaten into thin sheets and used for gilding certain objects. All such activities were under the direct supervision of scribes who recorded the weights to prevent the stealing of the precious metal usually brought from Nubia.

Beer was brewed from crumbled, lightly baked bread, sprouted grain, a starter (fermented remainder of old beer), a fruit for flavouring and water. The mash was left a few days to ferment and was then either eaten or filtered and consumed as a beverage. A number of beers are known by name and the difference between them may well be the added flavour. Dates were often used and tomb scenes show them being trampled in a large pot to produce a liquor for a certain type of beer.

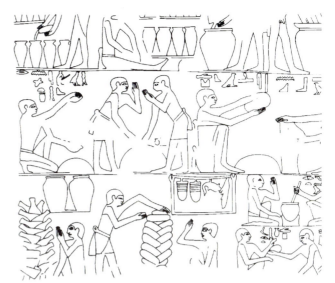

Leather Workers and Potters

Many other professions are shown in tombs, although less regularly. Leather workers are depicted stretching the hide and preparing it for the manufacturing of various objects, such as sandals and skin garments worn by priests and higher officials. In the New Kingdom they are also shown making military equipment, shields, quivers and certain parts of the chariots. As is the case today, the smell in such places must have been very unpleasant to the ancients, and the author of the Middle Kingdom Satire of Professions, Papyrus Sallier II, figuratively described the leather workers as 'he is well if one is well with corpses'. However,

Fig. 122 Making bread and beer, Pepyankh-heryib, Meir, Dynasty 6

*Fig. 123
Spinning and weaving,
Baqet, Beni Hasan,
Dynasty 11*

this pessimistic view of the author is general to all manual professions and aimed at enticing his son to study and become a scribe by painting for him a very dark picture of all other professions. Of the potter, for instance, he says 'the potter is under the soil, though as yet among the living. He grubs in the mud more than a pig, in order to fire his pots'. Potters at work were shown in tombs from the Fifth Dynasty onwards, the earliest being in the tomb of Ti at Saqqara, where the pots were produced by hand and also using the wheel. A scene in the Twelfth Dynasty tomb of Amenemhat at Beni Hasan shows men mixing the clay by treading it. The scenes also depict the kilns with men in front of them and protecting their faces from the heat with their hands. Brickmakers are also shown mixing earth, straw and water, then forming the bricks using moulds. The Theban tomb of Rekhmire of the Eighteenth Dynasty depicts all stages of brick making, including the drawing of water from a beautifully painted pond (fig. 80, pl. 63).

Spinning and Weaving

Spinning and weaving are also represented (fig. 123). Until the end of the Middle Kingdom this

profession was presumably reserved for women, as we see in the tomb of Khnumhotep at Beni Hasan, where the women are working crouching or seated on the ground. In the New Kingdom women were gradually replaced by men and because of the change in the type of looms they were able to work while standing. The products of the weavers were certainly in demand for both daily use and funerary purposes. Unlike spinning and weaving which took place in workshops, ropes appear to have been produced by boatmen, herdsmen, fishermen, etc., for their own use, although by the New Kingdom rope makers are shown with other craftsmen in workshops, as is the case for example in the tomb of Rekhmire at Thebes.

Bee Keeping

It is astonishing that in a civilisation like that of ancient Egypt, where sweet foods including honey were appreciated, where bees must have been common, and for some reason the bee was a symbol for the king of Lower Egypt, that scenes of bee hives are so rare. In the New Kingdom tomb of Rekhmire at Thebes two bee keepers are shown harvesting the honey, one man is collecting the honey combs from

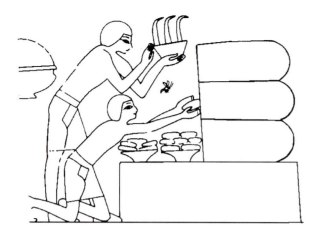

Fig. 124 Bee keeping, Rekhmire, Thebes, Dynasty 18

Pl. 48 Bee keeping, Pabasa, Thebes, Dynasty 26

Fig. 125 Receiving Gold of Honour, Ramose, Thebes, Dynasty 18

the opened back of the hive, while a second man holds a container with smoke to force the bees to fly out from the front of the hive and to drive them away. Two other men are shown pouring honey into storage jars (fig. 124, pl. 48).

Warriors

More distinguished careers were those of the army officers, physicians and above all, scribes. Nevertheless, scenes of training young recruits and of manufacturing war equipment such as chariots and bows and arrows, as in the tomb of Ipuia at Saqqara and Menkheperrasoneb at Thebes, are rare. While represented in royal temples, presumably to advertise certain victories, war scenes are also rare in private tombs. This was perhaps because they viewed victory as owing to divine aid and accordingly it was for the king to claim. However, some war scenes appear in private tombs, the earliest being in the tomb of Inti at Deshasha dated to the end of the Fifth Dynasty (fig. 139). It may be assumed that in such cases the tomb owners were not proclaiming any victory, but were proud of a certain role they played in the war, or of an honour they received from the king for their courage. In the tombs of the New Kingdom and although wars were not represented, many tomb owners are shown receiving the so-called 'Gold of Honour' for bravery. These awards consisted of heavy gold necklaces, armlets and bracelets (fig. 125).

Physicians

Many physicians are known from ancient Egypt, whether they own tombs or are portrayed in those of other higher officials. Yet apart from a few representations of operators manipulating the fingers and toes of customers and some manicure and pedicure scenes, only one instance of a surgical procedure is documented. The earliest example of finger and toe manipulation appears in the tomb of the two brothers Niankhkhnum and Khnumhotep in the Unis cemetery at Saqqara and dated to the latter part of the Fifth Dynasty. This seems a logical topic to represent in this tomb since both owners were royal manicurists. The same scene appeared again in two tombs of viziers, those of Ankhmahor and Khentika, in the Teti cemetery. Ankhmahor also shows the only surgical procedure depicted in a tomb, and accordingly it is locally known as the 'tomb of the physician'. Yet Ankhmahor curiously does not hold any title related to medicine, nor was he the operator, who is simply given the modest priestly title of 'Ka-servant'. It is also noticed that

100

no medical or surgical procedures of any kind appear in the contemporary and neighbouring tomb of Seankhuiptah, the 'Chief physician of Upper and Lower Egypt'. The operation depicted in Ankhmahor's chapel was generally taken to be circumcision, possibly of the tomb owner himself. Recently, the procedure has been interpreted as a treatment of paraphimosis, a condition of a swollen and infected foreskin which has retracted and can not be returned, interfering with the blood supply to the penis which may become gangrenous and may prove fatal. If so, then Ankhmahor did not only record a simple procedure, but a life saving operation (fig. 126).

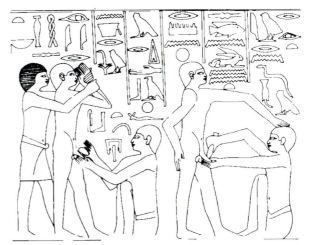

Fig. 126 Circumcision, Ankhmahor, Saqqara, Dynasty 6

Scribes

Scribes are commonly depicted in tomb scenes. They are shown counting and recording agricultural produce or the catch of fish and birds, inspecting animals, presenting accounts to the master, receiving accounts from farmers and herdsmen and presiding over the punishment of those who cheated, and so forth. While workers perform their duties in the open or inside workshops, scribes are usually shown seated with their scribal equipment under a canopy to protect them from the sun (fig. 127).

The Egyptian bureaucracy was particularly large and was responsible for the administration of various departments, the fields, the royal documents, the archive, the palace, the divine records, the army, etc. But on the whole, the position of scribes was regarded as the best of all professions in ancient Egypt. The author of the Satire of Professions says: 'There is no profession without a boss, except for the scribe; he is the boss'.

Market Scenes

As people were paid for their services in kind they needed to exchange what they received or what they produced for other necessities. Scenes of markets where both men and women bargain for different items of food, clothes, etc. are vividly recorded in

Fig. 127 Scribes at work, Hesi, Saqqara, Dynasty 6

tombs, and appear as a natural culmination to the nearby scenes of the production of these items. In the tomb of Ankhmahor at Saqqara the sellers are displaying baskets full of fruit and vegetables, bread loaves and even gutted fish. The scenes are frequently accompanied by a dialogue, and here the seller says: 'Look at these!', to which the buyer answers: 'Oh expert! You are a clever man' (fig. 128).

*Fig. 128
Market scene, Ankhmahor, Saqqara, Dynasty 6*

SPORT AND RECREATION

Pl. 49 Boxing, Kheruef, Thebes, Dynasty 18

Fig. 129 Girls playing, Baqet, Beni Hasan, Dynasty 11

*Fig. 130
Wrestling,
Baqet, Beni
Hasan,
Dynasty 11*

The Egyptian was no doubt very conscious of all the pleasures of life and wished to partake of them. Sports and games were for all age groups, and were enjoyed by the tomb owner as a participant or as a spectator. Fishing, fowling and hunting appear to be the sports the nobleman practised, but all kinds of other sports were represented as well in tombs. Children's games appear as early as the Old Kingdom in the tombs of Ptahhotep and Mereruka. The games are characterised by jumping, spinning round in a circle, balancing, mock combats, throwing darts at a target, and wrestling. As in all periods these children appear always vivid and active. Other games played by young men are also represented, such as boxing (pl. 49), fencing with papyrus stalks, even what seems to be yoga exercises. Such games continued throughout Egyptian history, yet in the Middle Kingdom more girls' sports are depicted, particularly ball-games. Young girls, with pigtails, are shown throwing and catching balls, or doing this while mounted on the backs of other girls (fig. 129). Juggling three balls in the air was also a familiar girls' amusement. Good examples of this are found in the Middle Kingdom tombs of Baqet and Khety at Beni Hasan. Wrestling also became especially popular among young men. The Middle Kingdom tombs at Beni Hasan display an overwhelming number of representations of different holds in a free-style wrestling. Varied modes of attack and defence were portrayed, and from these it appears that it was allowable to seize the adversary from any part of the body, including the head and neck (fig. 130). The fight seems to continue even after one or both had fallen on the ground. For clarity of movement to the viewer, the artist at Beni Hasan painted each two engaged wrestlers as one darker than the other. It has been suggested that the sequence of movements follow one another like a cinematographic reproduction. However, while all the holds are depicted, a hold does not seem to lead to the next and it is more likely that we have a large group of men playing or training simultaneously. As a result the rules of wrestling in ancient Egypt remain unclear to us. With the many wars in the New Kingdom, young men were trained in shooting with bow and arrows, but also in sports associated with fighting: boxing, wrestling and fencing with sticks as in the Eighteenth Dynasty tomb of Kheruef and the Nineteenth Dynasty tomb of Amenmose at Thebes. Boys and girls appear to have their separate games, but occasionally they played together. In the tomb of Baqet at Beni Hasan two men stood side by side and held the hands of two girls, who reclined backwards in opposite directions. The group then whirled around.

Music and Dancing

The Egyptian of the Old Kingdom seems to have preferred a quieter sort of entertainment. Either alone, or together with his wife or immediate family, he enjoyed food, music and dance. The typical musical instrument for such purposes was the harp, which was sometimes played for the man by his wife in a more intimate atmosphere, as in the tomb of Mereruka at Saqqara, or even by his daughters as in the tomb of Pepyankh-heryib at Meir (fig. 131). Women clapping rhythmically, as well as harp, flute and clarinet players accompanied the dancers, women or men, who performed separately. Although some of the women's dances required great flexibility of the body and ability to balance, as shown in the tombs of Ankhmahor (pl. 64) and Kagemni, the steps on the whole appear to be measured and rather restrained (fig. 132). During the New Kingdom changes in social habits are evident from tomb scenes, as for example that in the tomb of Rekhmire at Thebes. Proper banquets are now represented with large numbers of men and women guests. They were always dressed in the fashion of the period, including the necessary ornaments, cones of scented ointment on their heads, and frequently flowers in their hands. Servants, usually young men and women, attended to the guests' needs, helping them in their toilet or pouring them a drink, which they sometimes took to excess and are shown overcome by it. Entertainment became more sophisticated too, with musicians playing a number of instruments: harps, lyres, mandolins, single or double-pipe flutes and tambourines, with people clapping to provide the rhythm (pl. 50). Singers were often blind men, and dancers were young girls who twisted their almost naked bodies in what appear to be more flowing movements, with acrobatic elements sometimes introduced. Male dancers also performed, and Nubian men were employed for their folkloric dances. In these banquets, as is the case in the tomb of Rekhmire at Thebes, men and women seem to celebrate in separate quarters, each with their band of musicians and servants of the same sex (fig. 133). In general, the artists showed great vitality in women's parties and formality in those of men. There seems to be much more interaction and apparently more drinking in the women's quarters.

In pouring the drinks for the ladies, the servants say: 'For your Ka! Spend a happy day!'

Fig. 131 Playing the harp, Pepyankh-heryib, Meir, Dynasty 6

Fig. 132 Music and dancing, Nefer, Giza, Dynasty 5

Pl. 50 Musicians and dancers, Nakht, Thebes, Dynasty 18

103

Board Games

For a quieter type of entertainment the Egyptians, both men and women, enjoyed a variety of board games which are represented in tombs from all periods. The most popular of these games was called 'senet', which consisted of a board divided into thirty squares, over which were manoeuvered two sets of pieces of different shapes and colours. The game appears in many tombs as in that of Pepyankh-heryib of Meir (fig. 134) and was played by both men and women. Mereruka, Teti's vizier, presumably played it with his son (fig. 135). Scratched outlines of board games are also found on the floors of many tombs, as for example, those of Hesi and Inumin in the Teti cemetery at Saqqara. These may have been done by visitors to the tombs for their entertainment during the visits. Two men in the Middle Kingdom tomb of Baqet at Beni Hasan are shown playing a game with four cups. It is possible that one of the players concealed a ball under one of the cups, while his opposite party guessed its place.

FUNERARY RITES

A selection of the various episodes of the funerary procession is represented in some tombs from all periods. The theme first appeared in the Fourth Dynasty tomb of Debehni at Giza, but the better examples are recorded in the Sixth Dynasty tombs of Ankhmahor and Mereruka at Saqqara, Qar and Idu at Giza, Tjeti, Tjeti-iker and Kheni at Akhmim. One of the best preserved scenes, showing most of the episodes, is found in the Sixth Dynasty tomb of Pepyankh/Henikem at Meir (fig. 17), but this has to be complemented by the others, as none of the scenes shows all of the episodes. The same practices remained unchanged until the New Kingdom when scenes of the funerary procession were largely expanded, with the introduction of new elements, the most important of which was the actual depiction of the 'Opening of the Mouth', although the ceremony itself was mentioned as early as the Fourth Dynasty in the tomb of Metjen at Saqqara.

Embalming

Following the initial reaction to the death of a relative, the deceased body was taken to be ritually washed in the so-called 'purification tent' after which it was sent to the embalming workshop, usually on a bier carried by men.

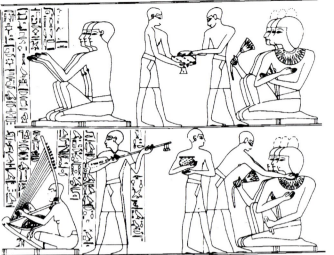

Fig. 133 Entertainment, Rekhmire, Thebes, Dynasty 18

Fig. 134 Playing Senet, Pepyankh-heryib, Meir, Dynasty 6

Fig. 135 Playing Senet, Mereruka, Saqqara, Dynasty 6

Accompanying the body was a procession of relatives, men and women, usually segregated, as well as some presumably hired professional mourners, a lector priest and an embalmer. Scenes, as those in the tombs of Ankhmahor and Mereruka from the Old Kingdom, show extreme expressions of grief. Men and women, who beat their faces and heads, smeared themselves with dirt, tore their clothes, fainted or threw themselves on the ground, are being supported by others and uttered lamentation cries, such as 'Oh! our father, our beloved!' or the like. Whether these scenes represent the feelings at the time the body was taken to be embalmed or later when it was taken to the tomb is uncertain, but the demonstration of grief would probably have been similar in both cases. The length of time the body spent in the embalming workshop depended on the means and importance of the deceased, with good mummification requiring approximately seventy days (see above).

What went on inside the workshop is never depicted in wall scenes, probably because it represented a sort of indignity to the corpse, the procedures involving cutting open the body and extracting most of its internal organs, before it was treated and wrapped (fig. 136). The last stages of bandaging and adorning appear, but rarely, in tombs of the Ramesside Period (fig. 137), as for example in those of Thay and Paser at Thebes. Yet the interpretation of such scenes remains uncertain. One even wonders if members of the deceased's family would have had the desire or the inclination to personally supervise or follow the actual progress of the process performed on their dear one. The lack of supervision could have been responsible for the confusion in the burial of Hefefi and his family at El-Hagarsa. With six members of one family - Hefefi and his wife, their son and his wife and two children - buried together in the same burial chamber, it appears that they died together. Evidence of bone injuries in most of the bodies suggests a traumatic death, presumably as a result of the internal fighting in the troubled period which accompanied the collapse of the Old Kingdom. The suddenly very busy embalmer made many mistakes of identity. Not only was the body of a man placed into a coffin inscribed for a woman and vice-versa, but also X-rays showed that a male face-mask was placed over a female body and the reverse. Of course the circumstances of this burial are unusual, but the fact remains that what took place inside the embalmer's workshop was secret, presumably even for the family and certainly not

Fig. 136 The embalmer's workshop, coffin of Djed-Bastet-iuef-anch, El-Hibeh, Ptolemaic

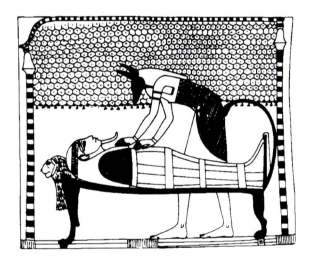

Fig. 137 Anubis and the mummy, Sennedjem, Thebes, Dynasty 19

for display. During the unsettled period which followed the fall of the Old Kingdom, the sage Ipuwer laments the situation saying: 'Lo, those who were entombed are cast on high ground. Embalmers' secrets are thrown away'.

Processions

A pilgrimage to Abydos is represented in many tombs and may have taken place after the completion of mummification and before the actual burial. Its purpose was perhaps to visit the sanctuary of Osiris, to take part in his festival, or even to be identified with him. Whether the voyage was real or fictitious, to be magically

Pl. 51
Grieving women, Ramose,
Thebes, Dynasty 18

Fig. 138
Rites accompanying
funerary meals, Pepyankh/
Henikem, Meir, Dynasty 6

Pl. 52
In the Field of Reeds,
Sennedjem, Thebes,
Dynasty 19

enacted in the future, is disputed. In such scenes the coffin, as in the tomb of Pepyankh/Henikem at Meir, or the tomb owner, rarely in Osirian form as in the tomb of Intefoker, appears in a papyrus boat towed by sailing boats or by men from the shore.

Returning the body to the deceased's house, the actual burial procession started. The coffin was carried by men who were followed by the mourners, men and women segregated (pls. 26, 51), and by servants and retainers carrying all the funerary possessions, which in addition to food and drink included clothing, furniture, precious belongings, etc. The procession then crossed the river by funerary boats to the west bank, where the coffin was either carried by men or placed on a sledge dragged by men or oxen as in the tombs of Idu at Giza and Tjeti at El-Hawawish.

The Opening of the Mouth Ceremony

The important ceremony of the 'Opening of the Mouth' which took place at the entrance to the tomb and which restored to the deceased his/her bodily functions is not represented in the Old Kingdom, although reference is made in the tomb of Neferseshemre in the Teti cemetery to 'making offering for him on top of his burial apartment in his house of eternity'. However, it is possible that such a ceremony was performed in this period upon the tomb owner's statue(s), before it left the sculptor's workshop to be placed in the tomb. During the New Kingdom the funerary procession was expanded, but the most important new element was the representation of the ceremony of the 'Opening of the Mouth' (pls. 26, 27).

Examples of the ceremony are found in the Eighteenth Dynasty tombs of Horemheb, Nebamun and Ipuky and Ramose at Thebes. Arriving at the entrance of the tomb, either the mummy in its anthropoid coffin or perhaps a statue was supported in a standing position by a priest sometimes wearing the head-mask of Anubis. Another priest holding four jars poured libation water four times over the mummy, the anthropoid coffin or the statue to purify it, representing the purification of Horus, Seth, Thoth and Sepa, while a lector-priest recited texts for the rite. A further priest burnt incense, and a sem-priest then touched the mummy on the mouth with some instruments, the most important of which is adze-like. Oxen were slaughtered and the foreleg of one was presented to the deceased to endow him with the ox's strength (fig. 20). Tomb scenes and more clearly the Book of the Dead on papyri, such as those of Any and Hunefer suggest that such forelegs were cut from living animals. Mourners are usually shown in the vicinity and the wife is depicted standing or kneeling at the feet of the mummy, obviously grieved by her loss. Since the tomb was decorated during its owner's lifetime, it is interesting that it was assumed that the wife would survive her husband. The mummy was then taken into the tomb, lowered into the burial chamber and placed into the sarcophagus.

Funerary Meal

A funerary meal followed and this was hoped to be repeated at every festival and every day. Many Old Kingdom tombs depict the preparations which accompanied the meal, including washing the hands, reciting rituals, censing, then at the end 'removing the footprints', where a priest is shown with a broom in hand sweeping the offering chamber (fig. 138).

Security

The security of the tomb and the mummy was of utmost importance. For this the sarcophagus had to be closed, the burial chamber sealed and the shaft filled with rubble. In some of the tombs in the Teti cemetery at Saqqara, where huge limestone sarcophagi with very large lids were placed in burial chambers, such as those of Ankhmahor, Kaaper and Khentika, an appeal was inscribed on the lids requesting the necropolis workers to properly close and seal the sarcophagi. Thus Ankhmahor, also known as Sesi, says:

> Oh 80 men, embalmer and administrator of the
>   necropolis and every
> functionary, who will descend to this place; do
>   you desire that the king
> favours you, that invocation offerings come to
>   you in the necropolis and
> your honour to be well before the great god, then
>   you should place for
> me this lid of this sarcophagus upon its mother
>   (i.e., its chest) as
> efficiently as you are able, as that which you
>   ought to do for an excellent
> spirit who did what his lord praised. I am the
>   beloved, Sesi.

IN THE HEREAFTER

Scenes of the afterlife are found in New Kingdom royal tombs, in the Book of the Dead and in many vignettes of this book depicted in New Kingdom tombs, particularly those at Deir el-Medina. The deceased, in many cases accompanied by his wife, was led by Anubis to the court of Osiris. On his way he could be received and judged by various other gods. In the court his heart was weighed against the feather of Maat, or Truth. Sometimes two hearts, those of man and his wife, were weighed together against two feathers, perhaps reflecting the desire to share the same lot in the Hereafter, or their joint responsibility for their actions on earth. The result was pronounced by Anubis and recorded by Thoth, who also declared it to Osiris. A composite monster was always waiting to devour the heart should it fail the test, yet the verdict seems always to have been in the deceased's favour (fig. 28).

Vignettes of the Book of the Dead depict the Gates of the Netherworld, which the deceased had to pass before arriving at the Judgement Hall. Following the judgement, the deceased and his wife would enjoy a perpetual life in the Field of Reeds, an evergreen, fertile land (pl. 52). Here they are shown working in agricultural pursuits, despite the fact that the ushabti-figures which were buried with them were supposed to act as a substitute in such manual labours. In the tombs at Deir el-Medina the owners and their wives are shown playing games of draughts in the Hereafter.

But the Egyptian view of the Hereafter, the Duat, is a very complex one. It is not restricted to life in the underworld, but also in the company of Re, who himself travels in the underworld at night, although in another myth he is swallowed by the sky-goddess Nut, who bends over earth, and travels inside her body to be born in the morning. Royal tombs of the New Kingdom show that the Duat was divided into twelve sections in accordance with the twelve hours of the night (figs. 26, 27). There the sun travelled backwards, from west to east, i.e., from death to birth. The sun god in his barque is shown traversing the underworld which is described and depicted, each section with its characteristics and dangers, until he rises again at the end of the journey.

INCIDENTAL THEMES

Scenes depicting important moments/events in the life of the tomb owner are rare in Old Kingdom tombs. Two such representations of the Egyptian army attacking fortified towns, probably in Syria/Palestine, are found in the tombs of Kaemheset at Saqqara and Inti at Deshasha. The two scenes are the earliest representations of an Egyptian campaign, probably in Asia and presumably commemorated for its magnitude and outcome. It is also likely that both Kaemheset and Inti played an important role in that expedition.

The better preserved scene in the tomb of Inti is very lively and full of action. Outside the fortified city, Egyptian archers, identified by their quivers, play a prominent role, with at least five depicted in the top register and one in the bottom register. From the posture of the last, it is obvious that he is aiming at men on top of the city walls, and some of them are actually shown falling, with as many as eight arrows transfixed in them. The second and third registers represented the Egyptian infantry with long handled battle-axes attacking opponents already wounded by arrows. This might reflect the inadequacies of the Egyptian bows and arrows of the time, for in the third register an Egyptian is attacking an Asiatic who was shot with six arrows yet was still able to break his bow, presumably in submission. The lower register depicts captives, old and young, roped together and led by Egyptian soldiers, one of whom carries a child over his shoulder. To the right two Egyptian soldiers, supervised by an overseer, are attempting to break through the enemy's fortified wall using long pikes, while another man adjusts a scaling ladder in preparation for storming the town. In Kaemheset's tomb men are instead using hoes to make a breach in the town wall.

Fig. 139 Attacking a Syrian fortress, Inti, Deshasha, Dynasty 5

108

Fig. 140 (top) Military activities, Khety, Beni Hasan, Dynasty 11
Fig. 141 (bottom) Military activities, Amenemhat, Beni Hasan, Dynasty 12

Inside the walls the enemy is panic-stricken. One man breaks his bow probably watched by his family, while another collapses as a woman attempts to remove an arrow lodged in his chest. The chief(?) of the city and one woman tear their hair in desperation, an old man defecates out of fear, while another man does the same presumably from the pain caused by an arrow in his buttocks. The middle registers show women attending to injured men, while in the bottom one the enemy is listening to the activities of the Egyptians trying to break through the fortified wall (fig. 139).

War scenes, like wrestling, were popular in the Middle Kingdom tombs of Beni Hasan. But unlike the Old Kingdom wars, these appear to be between two Egyptian camps; perhaps they represent clashes between neighbouring provinces around the time of the reunification of the country by Mentuhotep II and the establishment of the Middle Kingdom. Alternatively, these scenes might represent training in military activities (figs. 140, 141). They appear on the same walls with the wrestling activities and integrate well with them. Men are shown using spears, battle-axes, throw-

sticks, long pikes and bows and arrows. However, despite the fact that archers are shooting and men are falling from the fort, only one man seems to have received an arrow to his head and he is being helped by the archer himself. A few men lie in one area and it is uncertain whether they were dead, injured, or simply eliminated! But none of them has an arrow transfixed in him. The number of wrestlers, two hundred and twenty couples in the tomb of Baqet III alone, and the inclusion of wrestling and warfare on the same wall may well suggest that both themes were part of military training, and despite possible injuries in such training, the activities appear more staged than real and certainly lack the expected emphasis on the harm inflicted on an adversary. One of the very specific events is recorded in the tomb of Khnumhotep, governor of Beni Hasan, where he is shown receiving some foreigners clearly distinguished by their dresses and the style of their hair and beards. This is almost certainly a peaceful visit with the purpose of trade, establishing good relationships, or even settling in Egypt. The fact that a whole tribe appears to be represented,

Fig. 142
Delegation of
Asiatics,
Khnumhotep, Beni
Hasan, Dynasty 12

Fig. 143
Asiatics training
with Egyptians,
Amenemhat, Beni
Hasan, Dynasty 12

including its chief, men, women and children, seems to support the last alternative (fig. 142). In fact the papyri from Lahun clearly indicate the employment of Aamu (loosely translated as Asiatics) in the Middle Kingdom as house servants, but also in military and police units. Furthermore there were positions such as 'Officer in charge of Aamu troops' and 'Scribe of the Aamu'. In the war/military training scene in the tomb of Amenemhat at Beni Hasan a small number of what appears to be Aamu are shown but these should not be interpreted as enemies for they are training alongside the Egyptians (fig. 143). The delegation is presented to Khnumhotep by a royal scribe named Neferhotep, who delivers to the tomb owner an unrolled papyrus with inscriptions dating the event to the sixth year of the reign of Senusert II of the Twelfth Dynasty, identifying the visitors as Aamu, specifying their number as 37, and

mentioning the fact that they brought with them black eye-paint. In the scene they appear carrying other gifts as well.

In this same category of scenes we may also include the transportation of the colossus of Djehutihotep shown in his Twelfth Dynasty tomb at El-Bersha. The statue was cut from the alabaster quarries at Hatnub, secured on a sledge and dragged by 172 men arranged into 4 lines of 21 pairs and a leader each. Other men also took part, supervising the project, pouring a liquid in front of the sledge, perhaps ceremonially or to facilitate the movement of the sledge, carrying jars of water, burning incense to the statue, etc. (fig. 144). The inscriptions state that the colossus measured 13 cubits in height, which amounts to nearly 7 meters and must have weighed close to 60 tons. Although far bigger royal statues, made of granite and other hard stones, are known from ancient Egypt, this is

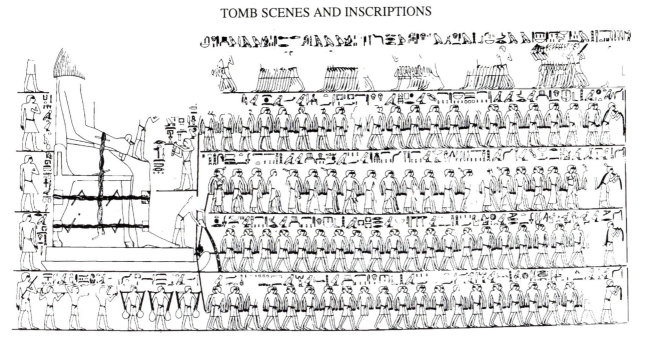

Fig. 144. Transportation of a colossus, Djehutihotep, El-Bersha, Dynasty 12

the largest single piece of alabaster recorded and it is curious that it belonged to a provincial governor rather than to a king. It is also questionable where such a statue would have been placed, for with its size it cannot fit inside a tomb, thus it was perhaps outside the tomb or a special chapel or even a local temple. The transportation of the statue to its final place must have required a great deal of organisation and preparation and the text refers to a stone (or perhaps rubble) road made especially for it.

During the New Kingdom, although the period was characterised by its military activities, scenes of warfare are lacking in private tombs. Such representations presumably became the prerogative of the kings and are commonly shown in their temples. However, a limited number of scenes exist in private tombs of the manufacturing of weapons, for example bows and arrows in the Eighteenth Dynasty Theban tomb of Menkheperrasoneb, and chariots in that of Ipuya at Saqqara. It is interesting to notice that nowhere was the army represented in private tombs as much as in those at El-Amarna. However, these are not scenes of warfare, but merely royal escorts. As Akhenaten and Nefertiti were regularly depicted in these tombs, so too were soldiers as well as chariots, perhaps needed for the protection of the royal family at a time of revolutionary changes.

New Kingdom officials represented in their tombs the highlights of their public life. Examples of this are found in the tomb of Rekhmire where he is shown accepting the office of vizier from King Thutmose III, and elsewhere receiving the tribute of various foreign lands. The themes of promotion and reward by the king became particularly popular in the Amarna period; there is hardly a tomb of a higher official which omitted such a theme. The vizier Ramose at Thebes showed the honours conferred on him in the form of gold collars and arm-rings. He also appears transmitting the king's commands to a group of foreign delegates (fig. 145). The tombs of Panehesy, Meryre, Parennefer, Tutu among others at El-Amarna depict the tomb owners receiving the

Fig. 145 Foreign delegates, Ramose, Thebes, Dynasty 18

Fig. 146
Decoration of the
burial chamber,
Ankhmahor,
Saqqara,
Dynasty 6

Gold of Honour from the king, and both Ay and his wife Tiy receive such honours from Akhenaten and Nefertiti. Almost all the tombs at El-Amarna also represent foreign delegations. Rewarding individuals with gold was known from the Old Kingdom, but became common in the New Kingdom. The rewards were for distinction in administration, in the army, or perhaps for mere loyalty. A change took place, however, in the Ramesside Period where the promotion and reward scenes became rare, and indeed the number of scenes of daily life in general reduced, giving way to representations of the Netherworld.

SIGNIFICANCE OF TOMB DECORATION

The Egyptian built his tomb as a dwelling for eternity. There, his mummy would be buried, his Ka would live forever, offerings would be presented to him with the necessary rites performed, his family and descendants would visit him and his deeds would be commemorated. He took every precaution to protect his body against decay by having it mummified, against vandalism by concealing it in a deep burial chamber and against both decay and vandalism by providing statues as substitutes either hidden in a closed chamber called a serdab, or shaped but left attached to the native rock in rock-cut tombs. Above the burial chamber he constructed a chapel which remained accessible to his priests and to visitors. In fact his image, usually depicted on the

façade or the entrance, and the accompanying inscriptions enumerating his good deeds and benevolent actions, aimed at inviting the passer-by to enter the tomb and present the owner with offerings, pronounce an invocation offering for him or merely mention his name. These inscriptions frequently promised the visitor with 'backing' in the Hereafter.

Both the burial chamber and the chapel were decorated whenever possible, although the decoration of the former seems to have been restricted to the top officials in the Old Kingdom, but became more common in the New Kingdom. The type of scenes depicted in the chapel and the burial chamber differed considerably, reflecting their treatment as two distinctive realms. The tradition of painting scenes in the burial chamber started at the end of the Fifth Dynasty, with Kaemankh's chamber, dated to the beginning of Djedkare's reign, probably being one of the earliest to be decorated. On the north wall of this chamber are scenes depicting sailing and transport ships (not those transporting the coffin), geese and other birds, the plucking and grilling of geese, the baking of bread and brewing of beer, and many storage jars. On the west wall scenes of agricultural activities and animal husbandry, stores, boat building (in very rough outline only) and pulling up the papyrus from the marshes are illustrated. The south wall shows the making of a bed, some furniture, music and dancing, the slaughtering of oxen, and heaps of offerings, while the east wall shows many offering bearers and an offering list. In the middle of the burial chamber, surrounded by

Pl. 53
Burial chamber,
Kaemankh, Giza,
Dynasty 5

Pl. 54
Burial chamber,
Kakherptah, Giza.
Dynasty 5

these vivid scenes of daily life, stands a large sarcophagus belonging to the tomb owner (pl. 53).

What makes the decoration of Kaemankh's burial chamber particularly interesting is that the themes depicted there have never been repeated in other burial chambers. A little later than Kaemankh, and in the vicinity of his tomb at Giza, Kakherptah constructed a mastaba, where he painted only the east wall of the burial chamber with his figure seated at an offering table and facing a long offering list of 100 items (pl. 54). From the reign of Teti, founder of Dynasty 6, the vizier Ankhmahor had painted on the north wall of his burial chamber an offering table, a heap of food items and a chair. But the chair was empty,

although the identity of its prospective occupant is beyond dispute because Ankhmahor's name and titles are written above it (fig. 146). Later burial chambers, if decorated, usually included scenes of food items of all sorts, cut and stacked, but not living creatures, humans or animals (pl. 64).

It appears, therefore, that after the initial attempt to decorate the burial chamber when it was treated as an extension of, or even a substitute for, the chapel, the idea of depicting living creatures in an underground room was quickly rejected. It is possible that the reason for this was to safeguard against any harm coming to the mummy in the future. If these creatures could be transformed through magic into living realities, they could

113

represent a threat to the deceased, which would defeat the very purpose of burial deep beneath the ground for greater protection. In the Pyramid Texts, inscribed in the burial chambers of kings and some queens starting from Unis, last king of Dynasty 5, and down to the end of the Old Kingdom, certain hieroglyphic signs, such as those of snakes, were also mutilated in order to render them harmless, and the same was done to the inscriptions in burial chambers of some individuals of the same period. However, the abandonment of scenes of daily life in burial chambers does not seem to have aimed simply at protecting the deceased, for in this case there would have been no need to eliminate his own figure. Thus it appears equally possible that the burial chamber being the realm of the dead was regarded as inappropriate for the depiction of activities related to life and the living.

The situation remained the same until the New Kingdom, when the burial chambers were decorated, for the first time, with scenes of the Hereafter. Vignettes from the Book of the Dead, showing such scenes as the deceased in the presence of the gods of the Netherworld and the weighing of his heart in the Hall of Judgement before Osiris, were now painted on the walls of the inner hall of the chapel, or in the burial chamber, or provided for the tomb owner in the form of a book on a papyrus roll, which was more common. The decoration of the chapel continued however to illustrate the life of the tomb owner, both private and public. The frequent representations of the funeral were not a departure from this situation, since it also took place on earth.

Originally, kings were seldom depicted in private tombs, but this started to change during the reign of Amenhotep III, and to a far greater extent during that of his son Akhenaten. In almost all private tombs, particularly those at El-Amarna, the king, the queen and often other members of the royal family dominate the scenes, dwarfing the figures of the tomb owner himself. Unlike earlier royal representations in private tombs, those at El-Amarna represent the king in all sorts of activities - on the Balcony of Appearance, rewarding his officials, riding in his chariot, enjoying a banquet, in the company of his family, kissing his children and so forth. He was also frequently shown performing religious duties, e.g., making offerings to certain gods, particularly Aten, but also Re-Horakhty, Atum and Hathor. The tomb owner was

then shown on a smaller scale, in a lower register, performing a similar action. All scenes of daily life, such as agriculture, fishing, fowling and industries, became very rare and those relating to the Hereafter are completely absent. We can hardly speak of the funerary beliefs of the Amarna period: Osiris and Anubis had disappeared with most other gods, and, judging by the scenes in private tombs of El-Amarna, there was a total reliance on the king during life and perhaps in the Hereafter. It is interesting that from this period we have the only representation of royal grieving, where Akhenaten and Nefertiti demonstrate their deep sorrow in front of the body of their dead daughter (fig. 14). Showing the human corpse is highly unusual in Egyptian art, except in battles and particularly when it applied to the dead enemy.

With the return of the court to Thebes at the end of the Eighteenth Dynasty and during the Ramesside Period, came a return to earlier traditions: the king was again represented sitting in a dignified position, although he continued to be shown rewarding his officials. From the Ramesside Period, the emphasis on scenes of daily life found in the pre-Amarna tombs diminished, being replaced by more scenes of the Hereafter. Furthermore, such scenes were not now restricted to the burial chambers and the inner hall of the chapel, but for the first time existed side by side with scenes of daily life in the outer hall. The Ramesside tombs at Deir el-Medina demonstrate this new development, which most probably reflects a change in funerary beliefs. The tomb appears now to represent the deceased's 'world', both on earth and in the Netherworld, without the clear distinction between them which existed earlier.

Because the Egyptian believed that his personality consisted of a number of different entities, it seems that he also believed that these took different paths in the Hereafter. Therefore, while only one entity lived in the Field of Reeds in the Netherworld, another remained in the tomb and was dependent for its survival on offerings from the world of the living, while a third entity was able to leave the tomb by day and enjoy the light. Thus, the arrangements the Egyptian made on earth for his afterlife were not extra precautionary measures in case he failed to gain access to the plentiful Field of Reeds in the Netherworld, but were absolutely necessary for the survival of the different entities of his personality.

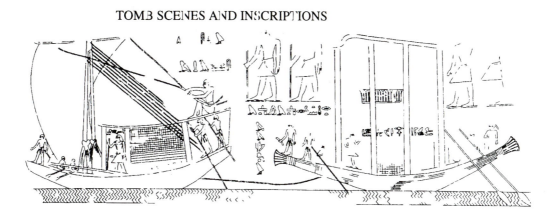

*Fig. 147
Funerary journey,
Kheni, El-
Hawawish,
Dynasty 6*

What was the significance of the scenes depicted in the burial chamber and the chapel, and in what way did they help the tomb owner in his afterlife? Certainly, the Egyptian believed that the spoken or the written word, the scene or the statue could be transformed through magical formulae into reality. It has been argued, therefore, that the traditional scenes of agriculture, animal husbandry, fishing, fowling, etc., would guarantee perpetual sustenance for the tomb owner. While this widely-held view is probable, other interpretations are equally likely. The most regular scene depicted in tomb chapels, and often the only one, was that of the tomb owner at an offering table laden with loaves of bread and sometimes other food items. In addition to being represented on one or more walls, this scene also occupied the central panel of the false door. If the walls of the chapel were left undecorated, the tomb owner or a relative provided a stela on which the owner was shown in the same position at the offering table (figs. 4, 10, 21). In most cases the scene was accompanied by an offering formula; 'An offering which the king gives and Osiris/Anubis (gives)... May an invocation offering come forth for (titles and name of the owner)'. Above the table was usually written: 'A thousand of bread, a thousand of beer, a thousand of fowl, a thousand of oxen, etc...'. The regularity of such representation, which appeared as early as the First Dynasty, demonstrates its importance for the deceased and suggests its funerary purpose. It was probably in front of this scene that offerings were presented and/or the formula was recited. As the deceased's Ka needed the body, a statue or even a sculpted or painted figure as its abode, it was possible for it to dwell in the seated figure in order to consume food offerings. Some false doors were provided with a statue of the tomb owner standing in the central niche, and an interesting substitute is found in the tomb of Idu at Giza, where a three dimensional bust of the deceased is cut in the lower part of the

central niche of the false door with the hands extended, palms up, on the offering slab in front of the door (pl. 15). This statue could house the Ka, emerging from the burial chamber through the shaft and the false door, to receive and consume the offerings. A most interesting and unusual false door is found in the tomb of Neferseshemptah in the Teti cemetery. There the outer jambs of the door were replaced by two deep niches each containing an engaged, standing statue of the tomb owner. A bust statue also appears in the central panel of the door (pl. 14).

The significance of the remaining scenes in the chapel is more questionable. Whether they were meant to be transformed into living reality, or were simply a commemoration of the environment, pleasures and achievements of the tomb owner, is uncertain. Because the tomb owner is always depicted watching the activities represented on the chapel walls, various theories have been put forward to explain his action. Some have argued that these activities took place in a Hereafter identical with this life. Not only did most of these activities never appear in scenes of the Netherworld which survive from the New Kingdom, but agricultural scenes, common to

Fig. 148 Female mourners (unfinished), Horemheb, Thebes, Dynasty 18

115

representations of both this life and the Hereafter, show major differences between the two. Furthermore, the fact that daily life activities were eliminated from the repertoire of scenes in the burial chambers after being documented in only one known example, that of Kaemankh, strongly argues against their being viewed as taking place in the Netherworld. If they were so considered, the burial chamber would have been the most suitable place for their depiction, as indeed it was for the final judgement of the deceased and his presence in the Field of Reeds.

Recognising the inappropriateness of the interpretation of such scenes as depictions of the Netherworld, scholars have offered alternative interpretations: that they represent posthumous visits to regions of the living, that they represent a symbolic domain to compensate the dead for actual loss; or that they are the summing up of a life's achievement; or, again, that they are the image of a man-in-death watching life's manifestations. The majority of opinions, therefore, agree that the activities shown in the tomb chapels took place on earth, and the idea that the picture of the tomb owner was that of 'a man-in-death watching life's manifestations' is based on his inactivity and the accompanying labels in hieroglyphs - e.g., 'Watching all the goodly work of the fields by (name of the tomb owner)', or the like. Yet the inactivity of the main figure was most probably not related to death, but meant to convey a posture of dignity, and certainly is not restricted to funerary art. Moreover, he could not be shown as active if what he is said to be doing is 'watching' one activity or another. When necessary, however, the tomb owner was depicted in an active posture,

though this was still subject to the rules of Egyptian art. Examples of this include scenes where he is shown spear fishing, fowling with a throw stick, holding the hands of his children, and playing a game of draughts, to name a few.

The scenes of the chapels depict the tomb owner during his lifetime, watching some activities and taking part in others. Some of these scenes are not narrative, in the sense that they do not refer to a specific event, time or place, but were regular activities and accordingly enjoyed by the tomb owner repeatedly during his life. The purpose of such representations in the chapel can only be conjectured. Since the chapel was the eternal house of the Ka, such depictions would create the surroundings with which the deceased was most familiar, and would be a perpetual reminder of his happy family relationships, his wife, his children at various ages, the sports and games he enjoyed, and proud moments of his career, such as a promotion, a reward, or a victory in war. Some of these scenes, as well as some biographical inscriptions, could also have been intended to impress his descendants so that they would present him with offerings, recite invocation offerings for him, or simply talk about him and mention his name. We should also bear in mind that only a selection of daily life activities are represented in any one tomb, probably according to the desire of the tomb owner or the artist's preference. If a harvest scene, for example, was capable of perpetually producing grain for the deceased, is it conceivable that any tomb owner, particularly those who owned richly decorated tombs, would have omitted it in his tomb? Furthermore, if the harvest scene was believed to magically turn into living reality, did

Pl. 55 Missing spear, Nakht, Thebes, Dynasty 18

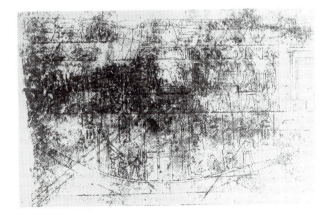

Pl. 56 Unfinished funerary scene, Pepyankh/Henikem, Meir, Dynasty 6

Pl. 57 (top) The work of Seni, Tjeti-iker, El-Hawawish, Dynasty 6
Pl. 58 (bottom) Shading, Seankhuiptah, Saqqara, Dynasty 6

Pl. 59 (top left) Musicians and dancers, Thebes, Dynasty 18, British Museum
Pl. 60 (top right) Birds in acacia, reproduction, Khnumhotep, Beni Hasan, Dynasty 12
Pl. 61 (bottom) Gathering fruit in a garden, Rekhmire, Thebes, Dynasty 18

Pl. 62 (top) Treading grapes, Nakht, Thebes, Dynasty 18
Pl. 63 (bottom) Brick makers, Rekhmire, Thebes, Dynasty 18

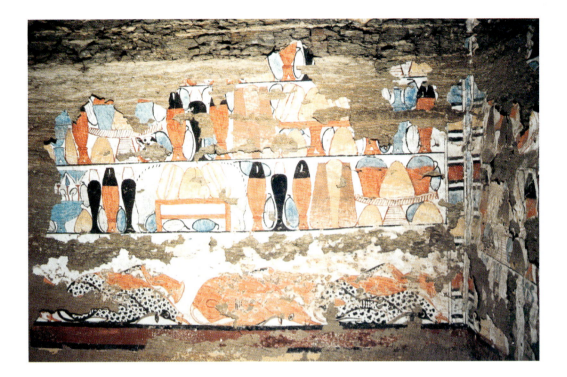

Pl. 64 (top) Burial chamber, Idut, Saqqara, Dynasty 6
Pl. 65 (bottom) Unfinished figure of owner, Nikauisesi, Saqqara, Dynasty 6

that also apply to the working peasants represented in the scene, even without their names recorded? On the other hand, if the representations did not have such a power, what was then the purpose of decorating the burial chamber with scenes of stacked food, and what was the reason for mutilating hieroglyphic signs depicting creatures, humans and animals? Yet at the same time how can we explain the fact that by far the majority of burial chambers in the Old and Middle Kingdoms, even those of well decorated tombs, were devoid of any scenes, if these scenes benefited the deceased? The problem is a complicated one and evidence in favour of each argument may be produced.

One of the more astonishing scenes found in some chapels is the so-called funeral scene/procession. This shows the various steps of the funeral, including the trip to the embalmer's workshop, the voyage to Abydos, the procession from the house of the deceased to his tomb, the ceremonies at the tomb entrance, and also depicts the lamentations of relatives and mourners. These activities are usually taken as representations of the actual funeral of the tomb owner, and they may well have been so. The following remarks express doubt rather than rejection of this interpretation.

The Egyptian has never represented himself in his own tomb as dead, i.e., a corpse, nor in the process of mummification. Rare scenes of bandaging, such as in the tombs of Thoy, Paser and Amenemope in Thebes, are known from the Ramesside Period, but the cadavers are completely wrapped. Considering that in each case a workman is shown chiselling some inscriptions on the wrapped figure, which is supported on two blocks rather than being placed on a bed, one wonders if these scenes show the actual wrapping of mummies or the manufacturing of the often similarly shaped anthropoid coffins. Similar 'mummies' appear in scenes of the 'Opening of the Mouth' ceremony, but even then the inscriptions indicate that the ceremony is performed on a statue, such as in the Theban tomb of Nebamun. Accordingly, it has been suggested that it is not the mummy which is depicted before the tomb but a statue in the form of a mummy (pl. 27). This opinion may also explain a number of problems associated with scenes of funerals. In some tombs two 'mummies' are seen in the ceremony, one with a beard representing the man, and one without representing his wife. But in other tombs, with joint owners, the two 'mummies' are bearded, as for example in the tomb of Nebamun and Ipuky. The concurrent ceremony involving the two

'mummies' presupposes the simultaneous death of the man and his wife, or of him and his tomb partner, which seems unlikely. Again, wives are frequently shown lamenting at the feet of the 'mummies', which presupposes the owner's expectation that his wife would survive him. Furthermore, in the tomb of Neferhotep at Thebes, from the reign of Ay, two similar 'mummies' are shown among the funerary furniture carried to the tomb. All these problems would be solved if these so-called 'mummies' were actually statues, and if the 'Opening of the Mouth' ceremony was performed on these during the owner's lifetime as part of his preparation of the tomb.

The often illustrated funerary procession presents another problem for, despite the depiction of the transportation of the coffin and the lamentation of the mourners, other evidence may hint that in some instances these were not the actual burial, but rather a kind of enactment, in which the coffin, obviously the most important piece of the funerary furniture and in which the body would rest, went through the same rites expected later for its owner. For this reason the coffin was accompanied by mourners expressing grief, as they also did in front of the statue in the 'Opening of the Mouth' ceremony. It is therefore possible that what is represented in both the funerary processions and the 'Opening of the Mouth' ceremonies were the empty anthropoid coffins on their way to be placed in the burial chambers. Firstly, the coffin is said to be taken to the purification tent and to the embalming place, but while these are depicted, frequently with priests inside, the deceased's body is never shown. The coffin is sometimes also shown being carried by too few men (for example three in both cases of Idu at Giza and Pepyankh/Henikem of Meir) to suggest that it contained the deceased's body. Furthermore, above the scene of transportation of the coffin in a boat in the tomb of Pepyankh/Henikem of Meir, the most complete of all funerary scenes, is written 'Behold, it is the escorting of the honoured one (to be repeated) a second time after a very happy old age' (fig. 17). In the tomb of Kheni at Akhmim the tomb owner himself is represented in the sailing ship towing his own funerary papyrus boat which could only happen if the procession took place during his lifetime (fig. 147). It should also be mentioned that placing the coffin in the burial chamber before the actual entombment would facilitate the introduction of the mummy down the shaft and into the chamber. Such a practice would have been inevitable in the case of the majority of tombs which possess massive limestone sarcophagi in their burial chambers. The lowering of such huge stone blocks to their destined places must have required very difficult and slow manoeuvres, which would have almost been impossible with the mummies inside them. In fact these large sarcophagi had to be lowered into the shafts even before the walls of the chapels were constructed. Confirmation of this comes from the tombs of Nikauisesi and Inumin in the Teti cemetery, where one of the chapel walls in each case was partly built on a beam above the shaft, reducing the size of its mouth and making it impossible for the sarcophagus to be introduced after the walls were built. Furthermore, the regular presence of a limited amount of limestone chips behind the sarcophagi in the burial chambers, for example in those of the Teti cemetery, suggests that the sarcophagi were lowered as rough blocks in which the chests were cut in the burial chambers. Such a technique would certainly avoid any major damage to the sides of the chest on its route from the quarries to the site and down the shaft to the burial chamber. While some mummies were directly placed in the stone sarcophagi, others were put in wooden coffins inside the sarcophagi or without the latter. However, the principle of lowering the coffin before the actual burial, if this principle existed, must have been commonly practised. Since the transportation of statues to the tomb was usually accompanied by the necessary ceremonies, it is reasonable to think that sarcophagi and coffins were equally treated and that in their New Kingdom anthropoid form enjoyed the 'Opening of the Mouth' ceremony.

The last point to be discussed here is that of the numerous unfinished scenes in tombs. It has been suggested in the first chapter that the late start on building one's tomb, and the slow progress of the work meant that many died before the preparation of their resting place was brought to completion, many of these being left totally uninscribed. Nevertheless, small sections of unfinished scenes, often only in outline, exist in numerous tombs where the decoration is otherwise perfectly complete. For all this to happen in each case as a result of the premature death of the owner seems highly unlikely. It has been proposed by some that much of the incompleteness was deliberate and for magical or superstitious reasons aimed at postponing the possible day of death, since once complete the tomb would perhaps be ready to symbolically receive its owner.

Whether this is correct is open to question, but what seems certain is that some scenes were deliberately left unfinished. It is hard to believe, for example, that the obviously missing spear in the spear fishing scene in the brilliantly painted tomb of Nakht at Thebes was an accidental omission (pl. 55). Interestingly, while the unfinished sections could exist in any part of the tomb and in any subject represented, many of them are found in scenes of the funerary procession. This may be seen, for example, in the Old Kingdom tombs of Tjeti of Akhmim and Pepyankh/Henikem of Meir (fig. 148), and in the New Kingdom tombs of Menna and Horemheb (pl. 56) of Thebes, and it is easy to see why a tomb owner would decide to leave this theme in particular unfinished. In the recently excavated cemetery of El-Hawawish at Akhmim it was noticed that an unusually large number of tombs of individuals who held the highest administrative posts in the province, such as that of governor, were left unfinished. Some of these scenes, or parts thereof, are left in red outline only, others have sections of the rock, often small, uncut and protruding from the native rock, yet the walls around them are plastered and decorated. It is also significant that none of the many tombs constructed/decorated by children or relatives of the tomb owners after their death has incomplete sections. The tomb of Nikauisesi in the Teti cemetery provides an interesting case; four rooms were completely decorated and one, into which the mouth of the main shaft opens, was left undecorated. On the thickness of the door to the last room is a figure of Nikauisesi, which is the only one incompletely carved in the whole tomb, yet it is coloured (pl. 65). In most cases the conclusion that the unfinished cutting or decoration was deliberate is inescapable.

These reflections on some problems related to the significance of tomb scenes are often speculative. While the tombs and their decoration provide us with a wealth of concrete information for a detailed study of various aspects of Egyptian life and death, it is much more difficult to penetrate the minds of ancient people and to understand their logic and symbolism. The study of these problems therefore has its limitations, but with continual archaeological discoveries and scholarly analysis and interpretation our understanding of the true beliefs of the ancient Egyptian is constantly enhanced and we draw closer to a more complete picture of his civilisation.

DEITIES MENTIONED AND THEIR ATTRIBUTES

Ammit

A hybrid monster represented in the weighing of the heart in the Netherworld. Usually depicted as a composite creature with the head of a crocodile, the forepart of a lion and the rear of a hippopotamus, waiting near the scales in the Hall of Judgement ready to gobble up the hearts should they fail the test against the feather of Maat.

Amun

Originally a local god of Thebes, Amun rose to prominence when this city became the capital of Egypt under Mentuhotep II at the end of the Eleventh Dynasty. His main temple was at Karnak, where he is described as 'king of the gods'. In order to maintain his popularity Amun had to combine with other powerful gods, such as Re, under the name Amun-Re. The name Amun presumably means 'the hidden one' and he was usually represented as a ram, or as a man wearing the double-plumed crown, frequently with projecting ram's horns.

Anubis

Anubis was believed to have been involved in the mummification of Osiris and hence became associated with embalming and with guarding the cemeteries. His common epithets summarise his attributes as: 'foremost of the divine booth, lord of the sacred land (necropolis), he who is upon his mountain, he who is in the embalming place'. He is represented as a reclining jackal or dog, often painted black, or as a man with this animal's head or a mask in this shape.

Aten

A form of the sun cult represented as a disc with rays ending with human hands. The Aten was growing in popularity during the New Kingdom, but was particularly favoured by Amenhotep III and fanatically so by his son Amenhotep IV/Akhenaten. The latter declared the Aten as sole god, built him a special temple at Thebes, then in year 5 decided to create a new capital, Akhetaten (El-Amarna), dedicated to the Aten. He also changed his name from Amenhotep to Akhenaten and started a persecution campaign against other deities, particularly Amun. Despite this, Akhenaten should not be considered as the first monotheist, for his main battle appears to have been against the growing power of Amun and his priesthood; yet the cult of other deities continued to be practised at El-Amarna itself, at least among the populace.

Atum

A form of the solar cult at Heliopolis, where he was associated with Re as Re-Atum. According to the Heliopolitan theology, Atum rose from the waters of the Nun on the Primeval Mound. He created the world by masturbating himself, resulting in two offspring, Shu (air) and Tefnut (moisture), who in turn produced Geb (earth) and Nut (sky) and in turn they produced Osiris, Isis, Seth and Nephthys. He was frequently shown as an anthropomorphic god with the double crown, and was believed to have protected the dead in their journey through the Netherworld.

Bes

Bes was represented as a naked, bow-legged dwarf with a big stomach and a large penis. Either his face, or a mask he wore, shows ferocious features, including a protruding tongue, a lion's mane and a plumed crown. He was believed to drive away evil and as such was considered as a protector of the family and was associated with sexuality and the protection of pregnant women and children. Bes was a popular deity and his image was painted on the walls of workmen's houses at El-Amarna and Deir el-Medina.

Hathor

An important goddess whose name means 'house of Horus' and accordingly was regarded as the divine mother of the king (Horus). She had many cult centres, the most important of which was Dendera, and also Memphis where she was designated as 'lady of the sycamore'. Hathor was also associated with foreign lands and accordingly was known as 'lady of Byblos' and at Sinai was 'lady of turquoise'. She was usually linked to sex and music and dancing, but also had funerary attributes, being 'the lady of the West', and as such the dead hoped to be 'in the following of Hathor'. She was represented as a cow or a woman with a headdress showing the ears and horns of a cow and frequently the sun disc.

Horus

According to the Osirian mythology, Horus was the son of Osiris and Isis. Following the murder of his father by his brother Seth, Horus defeated Seth, performed the ceremony of the 'Opening of the Mouth' to his father and claimed the right to inherit the throne. Horus became the embodiment of the Egyptian divine kingship. During his struggles with Seth, Horus injured his left eye, but the goddess Hathor was able to restore it. This became the 'wedjat-eye' or the sound eye of Horus, a common amulet. Horus was a sky god, represented as a falcon, or a man with a falcon head.

Isis

Isis was the sister-wife of Osiris and the mother of Horus. She was the faithful wife who collected the parts of her husband's body, after he was murdered by Seth, and mummified him, with the help of Anubis, and hovered like a kite over the mummy, magically conceiving Horus. She was worshipped in a number of sites inside Egypt, particularly at Philae and Dendera, and outside Egypt, e.g. at Byblos. She is frequently represented as a woman suckling Horus the child. As such, she was connected with Hathor and was occasionally shown with the Hathorian horns and sun disc.

Khnum

Khnum was shown as a ram and later as a man with a ram's head. His main cult centre was the island of Elephantine at Aswan, where he was regarded as guardian of the source of the Nile and responsible for the inundation. His association with the Nile and the fertile soil contributed to his image as a potter who fashioned the children on a potter's wheel and implanted them into their mother's bodies. He also assisted at childbirth. His best preserved temple is at Esna, where he is described as the creator of all beings.

Maat

Believed to have come into being at the moment of creation, Maat was considered as the daughter of Re. She personified justice, truth, order and harmony, and accordingly shaped the responsibilities of kings and judges and people had to account to her when they died. She was represented as a woman with an ostrich feather attached to the head, or simply as the feather itself, and it is this symbol that was placed in the scales against the heart of the deceased in the Hall of Judgement.

Min

Min was a god of fertility who bestowed sexual powers in man and generative force in nature, particularly the growth of grain. His main cult centres were at Koptos and Akhmim and he was usually represented as a mummified male with an erect phallus and one raised arm carrying a flail. He wore a crown with two plumes and a ribbon that falls behind his back.

Nephthys

She was the sister of Isis and the wife of Seth. Because of her association with Isis and help to Osiris, she was later considered the mother of Anubis by Osiris himself. Nephthys had no cult centres of her own and she was represented as a woman with the signs for her name, which means 'Lady of the Mansion', above her head.

Nun

Nun was a deity symbolising the original ocean of chaos from which the Primeval Mound and Atum appeared. The Nun continued to represent the place for condemned spirits and the deepest part of the Netherworld.

Nut

She was the daughter of Shu, the sister-wife of Geb and the mother of Osiris, Isis, Seth and Nephthys. She was depicted as a woman, or less commonly a cow, arched over the god of the earth, Geb. Each evening she swallowed the sun which travelled in her body to be born again the next morning. This journey is shown on the ceilings of temples and royal tombs at Thebes. Nut's belly was also the course of the stars and was regularly decorated with these on the ceilings.

Osiris

One of the oldest and most important gods of Egypt, who was also believed to have been an early ruler of the country, Osiris was murdered by his brother Seth. With the help of his wife Isis he conquered death, was resurrected and became god of the dead, while his son, Horus, ruled Egypt. His main cult centres were Busiris in the Delta and Abydos in Upper Egypt, in the former it was believed that his backbone (the Djed pillar) was buried, while in the latter it was his head. He was represented as a mummified man holding the crook and flail and wearing the atef crown. Because of his resurrection, Osiris became also identified with fertility and as such his skin was painted black to represent the earth or green to represent rejuvenation.

Ptah

This god was believed to have created the world through the words which came from his tongue. He was also associated with crafts and craftsmen. His main centre was Memphis and he was represented as a mummified man, sometimes with a straight beard, holding a staff terminating with the signs for stability, life and dominion. From the Old Kingdom he became associated with the Memphite hawk-god, Sokar, under the name Ptah-Sokar and in the Late Period with Osiris under Ptah-Sokar-Osiris.

Re

Re was the most universal deity of Egypt, with one of the royal titles being 'Son of Re'. His cult came to a particular prominence in the Fifth Dynasty with each king building a Sun-temple. However, Re never lost importance and many other gods were later associated with him, such as Amun-Re, Montu-Re, Atum-Re, Re-Osiris, even Horus became Re-Horakhty. Re's main cult centre was Heliopolis and he was represented as a hawk-headed man with a sun-disc headdress. In the Netherworld journey he appears ram-headed.

Renenutet

Represented as a cobra-goddess, Renenutet was responsible for fertility and harvest and thus was described as 'lady of the fertile land' and 'lady of granaries'. During the harvest seasons people presented offerings to her image, but she was particularly concerned with the nourishment of children.

Sepa

Worshipped at Memphis, Sepa was a minor god whose name means 'centipede'. He was connected with the necropolis and had power against harmful animals and enemies of the gods.

Sons of Horus

These are Hapy, Duamutef, Qebehsenuf and Imsety, who were each responsible for the protection of a particular internal organ of the deceased. Represented as the head of a man, a jackal, a baboon and a hawk, their figures were used from the New Kingdom onwards as stoppers of the four canopic jars.

Taweret

Taweret was shown as a pregnant hippopotamus standing upright with pendular breasts. She was helpful to women during childbirth and accordingly often held the sa-sign of protection or the ankh-sign of life. No temple is known for Taweret, but many statues and representations of the goddess were found. Amulets of Taweret were used from the Old Kingdom onward and some were found in the houses at El-Amarna.

Thoth

Thoth was the god of writing and knowledge and as such he appeared in scenes of the judgement of the dead, as shown in the Book of the Dead, recording the results of the process of weighing the heart against the feather of Maat. His main cult centre was Khmun in Middle Egypt and he was represented either as an ibis-headed man holding the scribal equipment or less commonly as a baboon.

LIST AND SOURCES OF FIGURES AND PLATES

Line drawings are listed as figures, while photographs are listed as plates. All figures have been drawn or redrawn for the present publication, with the source given after each figure. All drawings of scenes and inscriptions were produced by Mr. Sameh Shafik, while architectural plans and sections were done by Mr. Naguib Victor. Unpublished figures are from current projects by the author. Most of the plates are from the author's excavations and his personal collection. The photographs for the cover and plates 10, 11, 20, 29, 30, 41, 42, 47-52, 55, 61-63 were kindly supplied by Mrs. Leonie Donovan, plates 23-26, 28, 31, 59 by the British Museum, plates 5, 12, 14, 21, 22 by the Egyptian Museum, Cairo and plate 16 by the Museum of Ancient Cultures, Macquarie University.

FIGURES

PLATES

BIBLIOGRAPHY

Andrews, C., *Egyptian Mummies* (London, 1984).

Badawy, A., *A History of Egyptian Architecture*, 3 vols. (Cairo/Los Angeles, 1954-68).

Baines, J. - Málek, J., *Atlas of Ancient Egypt* (Oxford, 1980).

Bard, K. A. (ed.), *Encyclopedia of the Archaeology of Ancient Egypt* (London, 1999).

Baumgartel, E., *The Cultures of Prehistoric Egypt* (Oxford, 1960).

Beckerath, J. von, *Chronologie des pharaonischen Ägypten: Die Zeitbestimmung der ägyptischen Geschichte von der Vorzeit bis 332 v. Chr.* (Mainz/Rhein, 1997).

Bierbrier, M. L., *The Tomb-Builders of the Pharaohs* (London, 1982).

Blackman, A. M., *The Rock Tombs of Meir*, 6 vols. (London, 1914-53).

Bourriau, J. D., *Pharaohs and Mortals: Egyptian Art in the Middle Kingdom* (Cambridge, 1988).

Brunner-Traut, E., *Altägyptische Märchen* (Dusseldorf, 1976).

Brunton, G. - Caton-Thompson, G., *The Badarian Civilisation and Predynastic Remains Near Badari* (London, 1928).

Budge, E. A. W., *The Book of the Dead* (London, 1969, repr.).

Cerny, J., *Ancient Egyptian Religion* (London, 1952).

D'Auria, S. - Lacovara, P. - Roehrig, C. H. (eds.), *Mummies and Magic: The Funerary Arts of Ancient Egypt* (Boston, 1988).

David, A. R. (ed.), *The Manchester Museum Mummy Project* (Manchester, 1979).

David, A. R. - Tapp, E. (eds.), *Evidence Embalmed* (Manchester, 1984).

Davies, N. de G., *The Mastaba of Ptahhetep and Akhethetep at Saqqareh*, 2 vols. (London, 1900-1901).

Davies, N. de G., *The Rock Tombs of Deir el-Gebrâwi*, 2 vols. (London, 1902).

Davies, N. de G., *The Rock Tombs of El-Amarna*, 6 vols. (London, 1903-1908).

Davies, N. de G., *The Tomb of the Vizier Ramose* (London, 1941).

Davies, N. de G., *The Tomb of Rekh-mi-Re at Thebes* (New York, 1943).

Davis, W., *The Canonical Tradition in Ancient Egyptian Art* (Cambridge, 1989).

Duell, P., *The Mastaba of Mereruka*, 2 vols. (Chicago, 1938).

Eggebrecht, A., *Suche nach Unsterblichkeit Totenkult und Jenseitsglaube im Alten Ägypten* (Hildesheim, 1990).

Emery, W. B., *Archaic Egypt* (Harmondsworth, 1961).

Épron, L. - Wild, H., *Le tombeau de Ti*, 3 fascs. (Cairo, 1939-66).

Faulkner, R. O., *The Ancient Egyptian Book of the Dead*, ed. by C. Andrews (New York, 1972).

Fisher, C. S., *The Minor Cemetery at Giza* (Philadelphia, 1924).

Gaballa, G. A., *Narrative in Egyptian Art* (Mainz/Rhein, 1976).

Gardiner, A. H., *Egyptian Letters to the Dead, Mainly from the Old and Middle Kingdoms* (London, 1928).

Gardiner, A. H., *The Attitude of the Egyptians to Death and the Dead* (Cambridge, 1935).

Garstang, J., *Burial Customs of Ancient Egypt* (London, 1907).

Groenewegen-Frankfort, H. A., *Arrest and Movement: An Essay on Space and Time in the Representational Art of the Ancient Near East* (New York, 1972).

Hassan, S., *Excavations at Gîza*, 10 vols. (Oxford/Cairo, 1929-60).

Herodotus, *The Histories*, translated by A. de Sélincourt, revised by A. R. Burn (Harmondsworth, 1972).

Hornung, E., *Tal der Könige: Die Ruhestätte der Pharaonen* (Zurich, 1982).

Hornung, E., *Die Nachtfahrt der Sonne. Eine altägyptische Beschreibung des Jenseits* (Zurich/Munich, 1991).

Ikram, S. - Dodson, A., *The Mummy in Ancient Egypt: Equipping the Dead for Eternity* (London, 1998).

James, T. G. H., *An Introduction to Ancient Egypt* (London, 1979).

James, T. G. H., *Pharaoh's People: Scenes from Life in Imperial Egypt* (Oxford, 1984).

Jéquier, G., *Tombeaux de particuliers contemporains de Pepi II* (Cairo, 1929).

Junker, H., *Grabungen auf dem Friedhof des Alten Reiches bei den Pyramiden von Gîza*, 12 vols. (Vienna, 1929-55).

Kanawati, N. *The Rock Tombs of El-Hawawish: The Cemetery of Akhmim*, 10 vols. (Sydney, 1980-92).

Kanawati, N., *The Tomb and its Significance in Ancient Egypt* (Cairo, 1987).

Kanawati, N., *The Tombs of El-Hagarsa*, 3 vols. (Sydney, 1993-95).

Kanawati, N. - Scannell, R., *A Mountain Speaks: The First Australian Excavation in Egypt* (Sydney, 1988).

Kanawati, N. - McFarlane, A., *Deshasha: The Tombs of Inti, Shedu and Others* (Sydney, 1993).

Kanawati, N. et al., *The Teti Cemetery at Saqqara*, 6 vols. (Warminster, 1996 -).

Koch, K., *Geschichte der Ägyptischen Religion* (Cologne, 1995).

Lange, K. - Hirmer, M., *Egypt: Architecture, Sculpture, Painting in Three Thousand Years* (London, 1956).

Lexikon der Ägyptologie, 7 vols., eds. W. Helck - E. Otto - W. Westendorf (Wiesbaden, 1972-1992).

Lichtheim, M., *Ancient Egyptian Literature: A Book of Readings*, 3 vols. (Berkely, 1973-80).

Lucas, A., *Ancient Egyptian Materials and Industries* (4th edition, London, 1962).

Macramallah, R., *Le mastaba d'Idout* (Cairo, 1935).

Martin, G. T., *The Royal Tomb at El-'Amarna* II (London, 1989).

McFarlane, A., *The Unis Cemetery at Saqqara*, vol. I (Warminster, 2000).

Mekhitarian, A., *Egyptian Painting* (London, 1978).

Muhammed, M. A., *The Development of the Funerary Beliefs and Practices Displayed in the Private Tombs of the New Kingdom at Thebes* (Cairo, 1966).

Newberry, P. E., *El-Bersheh*, 2 vols. (London, 1893-94).

Newberry, P. E. et al., *Beni Hasan*, 4 vols. (London, 1893-1900).

Ockinga, B. - Al-Masri, Y., *Two Ramesside Tombs at El-Mashayikh* (Sydney, 1988-90).

Ockinga, B., *A Tomb from the Reign of Tutankhamun at Akhmim* (Warminster, 1997).

Peet, T. E., *The Great Tomb Robberies of the Twentieth Egyptian Dynasty*, 2 vols. (Oxford, 1930).

Reisner, G. A., *A History of the Giza Necropolis*, vol. I (Cambridge, MA, 1942).

Robins, G., *Proportion and Style in Ancient Egyptian Art* (London, 1994).

Roccati, A., *La littérature historique sous l'Ancien Empire Égyptien* (Paris, 1982).

Romano, J. F., *Death, Burial and Afterlife in Ancient Egypt* (Pittsburgh, 1990).

Schäfer, H. (translated by J. Baines), *Principles of Egyptian Art* (Oxford, 1974).

Shaw, I. - Nicholson, P., *British Museum Dictionary of Ancient Egypt* (London, 1995).

Shedid, A. G., *Das Grab des Sennedjem* (Mainz/Rhein, 1994).

Simpson, W. K. (ed.), *The Literature of Ancient Egypt* (New Haven, 1973).

Simpson, W. K., *The Mastabas of Qar and Idu: G7101 and 7102* (Boston, 1976).

Smith, M., *The Liturgy of Opening of the Mouth for Breathing* (Oxford, 1993).

Smith, W. S., *The Art and Architecture of Ancient Egypt* (Harmondsworth, 1965).

Smith, W. S., *A History of Egyptian Sculpture and Painting in the Old Kingdom* (New York, 1978).

Spencer, A. J., *Death in Ancient Egypt* (Harmondsworth, 1982).

Spencer, J. (ed.), *Aspects of Early Egypt* (London, 1996).

Strouhal, E., *Life in Ancient Egypt* (Cambridge, 1992).

Vandier, J., *Mo'alla: La tombe d'Ankhtifi et la tombe de Sebekhotep* (Cairo, 1950).

Vandier, J., *Manuel d'archéologie égyptienne*, 6 vols. (Paris, 1952-78).

Zâbkar, L. V., *A Study of the Ba Concept in Ancient Egyptian Texts* (Chicago, 1968).

INDEX

DIETIES

numbers in italics are the the entries in the section of deities mentioned and their attributes

KINGS and QUEENS

PERSONAL NAMES